Winemaking at home

Heinz and Geneste Kurth
WINEMAKING
at home

B. T. BATSFORD LTD., LONDON

Acknowledgements: special thanks to Pat Simon M.A., M.W. for his help in clarifying many features of the winemaking process and for passing on his wine tasting notes shown on page 50; and to H. Kurth's father who introduced him to the art of making wine as well as tasting it in the family's vineyard.

Created and produced by Ventura Publishing Ltd., 44 Uxbridge Street, London W8 7TG

ISBN 0 7134 4027 9

Filmsetting by Oliver Burridge and Company Limited, Crawley, Sussex
Colour origination by D. S. Colour International Limited, London
Printed in Spain

contents

6

The dawn of viniculture

Winemaking, or viniculture, is a very ancient pursuit. According to legend, it began when Noah left his ark and at once planted a vineyard which helped him to live happily for a further 350 biblical years. But archaeologists also believe that neolithic man was probably fermenting mead or wine as long as 10,000 years ago as a rather more healthy alternative to the unpalatable bogwater available to him. Certainly, stone reliefs show that grape vines were being cultivated by 2000 BC in Egypt, Mesopotamia and Greece: they were trained in the shape of pergolas, much the same way as they are grown today in certain regions.

By Homeric and later Roman times, the Mediterranean had become the natural home of winemaking. The basis of communal existence in those days was the Mediterranean triad: wheat, the olive and the vine. Cultivating the three together was a system that supplied almost everything that was needed for living – excluding meat, but that was scarce and not commonly eaten. The system has endured in some places to this day: in modern Portugal, for instance, vines are still trained up tall trees around the fields, while in Tuscany they are looped between olive-trees while wheat is planted between the vines – each of the three crops taking different minerals out of the rocky soil and using the available water during different months of the year.

When Greek, and later Roman administrators planted vineyards as well as wheat and barley fields in many of their 'dominions' in north Africa, Spain, France and Britain, winemaking spread and by the twelfth century many vineyards now well-known were already established in Rhenish and Burgundian districts. Since land transport was often difficult and dangerous, most of the vineyards were situated near rivers, which were the best means of communication. Barges could take the wine in animal skins or wooden casks down the Rhine, Garonne, Gironde and Loire to the Low Countries, and thence to Scandinavia and Britain. The vineyards themselves were usually small enough to be run by a farmer and indeed much of today's wine is still produced on holdings no larger than five acres.

In the seventeenth century, glass wine bottles and corks became common and an important discovery was made in the Rheingau: grapes that were left to become overripe on the vine developed an *Edelfäule* or 'noble rot' which alone produced the great Hocks and Sauternes. At about the same time, shippers in Madeira began to add brandy to their wines so that they would remain stable during prolonged sea-journeys – a practice also later adopted for Portuguese wines, the 'ports'.

Egyptian grape press

Opposite page: early wine containers were made of animal skins (1) or animal horns (2) but the most telling historical evidence comes from durable man-made materials such as fired clay, china or glass. (3) Franconian neolithic clay flask c.3000 BC; (4) Egyptian amphora c.1800 BC; (5) Cretan clay jar c.1500 BC with typical octopus pattern; (6) Chinese bronze wine vessel c.1000 BC; (7) Greek clay psykter c.500 BC – a wine cooling jar; (8) Etruscan clay jar c.500 BC; (9) golden amphora c.300 BC from Thrace; (10) bottle made from blown glass c.200 AD from Syria; (11) Rhenish glass bottle c.300 AD; (12) pilgrim bottle c.1250 from Syrian glass; (13) Chinese flask c.1400; (14) French clay jar c.1560; (15) Dutch glass bottle c.1650; (16) one of the earliest port bottles c.1710; (17) American stoneware jug c.1830; (18) American mould-blown glass bottle 'Frigate Mississippi' c.1850; (19) English decanter c.1850; (20) English ship's decanter c.1870; (21) modern decorated African gourd bottle; (22) port bottle; (23) German 'Boxbeutel' for Franconian wines; (24) Italian 'Chianti' bottle; (25) French Alsace; (26) Bordeaux bottle; (27) Burgundy bottle; (28) German Rhine wine; (29) German Moselle bottle.

What is wine?

The word 'wine' is usually understood to mean grape wine (from the Greek word *oinos*), which is the fermented juice of the fruit containing the seed of the vine plant, the grape. Beverages made from fruit or other ingredients carry the word 'wine' with no justification other than convenience, mainly because the more accurate description 'fermented fruit juice' is not a very attractive one. Another euphemism, 'country wine', also seems inappropriate these days for wine that may be made on the eighth floor of a town building with ingredients bought at a supermarket. The simplest way of defining a fruit wine is by its main ingredient 'apple wine', 'plum wine' and so on.

Grape wine embraces a wide range of alcoholic beverages which are drunk before, with and after meals. According to custom, light dry wines, dry sherries or apéritif wines are taken before the meal; dry red or white wines with the main course; sweet dessert wines with sweet after-courses; fortified wines such as port with cheese; and so-called 'social wines' such as sweet sherries or Madeira after the meal.

The difference in colour between red and white wines does not result directly from using either black or white grapes. Red wines are made by *including* skin, pips and stems with the juice, from which colouring matter leaches out into the must during fermentation of the pulp. White wines, on the other hand, are made from either black or white grapes but if black grapes are employed, only their colourless juice is extracted in a press while the skin etc. is *removed* before juice fermentation takes place.

Wines are either dry (when almost all the sugar has been fermented out) or sweet, (when fermentation has been ended before its natural completion so that a trace of sugar remains in the wine). 'Fortified wines' are wines to which alcohol has been added so that they are stronger in body, more stable and last longer. Normally, however, the grape supplies all the necessary ingredients including sugar, acids and a host of minerals, all of which contribute to its alcohol content, flavour, body and aroma. This is what distinguishes it from other types of fruit which usually lack one or more of the elements which the grape has in abundance. Fruit wines usually need to have sugar added, plus small amounts of other minerals in order that they will ferment satisfactorily and produce the required amount of alcohol.

Alcohol gives body to a wine: without it the liquid would be just fruit juice. Alcohol also inhibits bacterial infection and stabilises the wine so that it can be kept in bottles for many years. The proportion of alcohol in a wine can be determined either in per cent by volume or as 'proof spirit'. The latter is a very outdated, misleading and needlessly complicated way of describing alcohol content based on the British 1952 Customs and Excise Act according to which 100% pure alcohol is 175 proof spirit.

	alcohol by volume	British proof	U.S. proof
Table wines	10 – 16%	17 – 28	20 – 32
Fortified wines	17 – 25%	29 – 44	34 – 50
Spirits	40% or more	70 or more	80 or more

To help the reader who wants to convert one into the other, a rough conversion factor is 4/7. So if a given spirit is 70 proof, for instance, divide 70 by 7 and multiply the result by 4, and the answer is 40% alcohol by volume. Conversely, to convert alcohol by volume into British proof, the factor is 7/4. Therefore 80% alcohol is 140 proof and the authors would love to know where to buy it!

The American authorities re-defined 100% alcohol by volume as 200 U.S. proof spirit, which is easier to work out since it means that U.S. proof is always double the percentage of alcohol by volume.

8

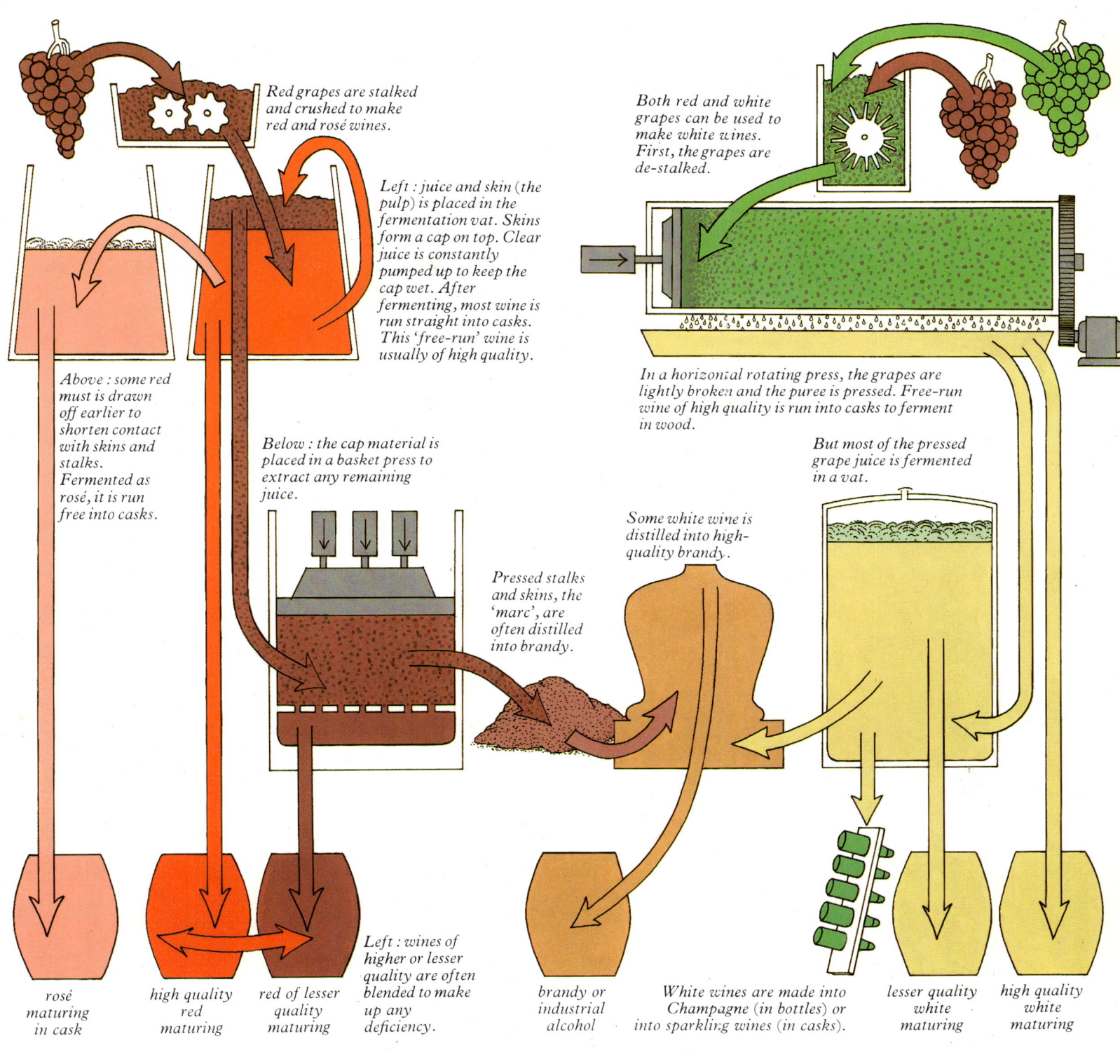

Red grapes are stalked and crushed to make red and rosé wines.

Both red and white grapes can be used to make white wines. First, the grapes are de-stalked.

Left: juice and skin (the pulp) is placed in the fermentation vat. Skins form a cap on top. Clear juice is constantly pumped up to keep the cap wet. After fermenting, most wine is run straight into casks. This 'free-run' wine is usually of high quality.

Above: some red must is drawn off earlier to shorten contact with skins and stalks. Fermented as rosé, it is run free into casks.

In a horizontal rotating press, the grapes are lightly broken and the puree is pressed. Free-run wine of high quality is run into casks to ferment in wood.

Below: the cap material is placed in a basket press to extract any remaining juice.

But most of the pressed grape juice is fermented in a vat.

Some white wine is distilled into high-quality brandy.

Pressed stalks and skins, the 'marc', are often distilled into brandy.

Left: wines of higher or lesser quality are often blended to make up any deficiency.

rosé maturing in cask

high quality red maturing

red of lesser quality maturing

brandy or industrial alcohol

White wines are made into Champagne (in bottles) or into sparkling wines (in casks).

lesser quality white maturing

high quality white maturing

Wine-drinking today

With the exception of polar regions, vines will grow almost anywhere in the world but grapes intended for winemaking need warmth and sunlight to enable them to ripen fully. The plants also require moderate winters in which to rest and restore their strength for the coming fruiting season. The best conditions for this exist in the two zones between 30° and 50° in the northern and southern hemispheres.

Generally good climatic conditions, coupled with centuries of experience, have meant that nearly three quarters of the world's wine is made in Europe, but other countries are increasing production.

Since many types of fruit and berries will grow in adverse conditions which would not suit grapes, fruit wines can be made much further north and south than grape wines and the amount of fruit wine produced by commercial and private winemakers every year is greater than is generally realised.

Today, more people than ever before drink and enjoy wine. In moderation, it is beneficial to health; it is a sedative and a relaxant which calms overwrought nerves and soothes minor aches and pains. Most of all, though, wine is a delicious accompaniment to a meal. About 42,000 million bottles of grape wine alone are produced and consumed every year – two dozen bottles or more for every man and woman on this planet.

However, as more people than ever before appreciate wine, it has become increasingly difficult and expensive to buy the better vintages. Inflation too has contributed towards putting the daily glass or two of wine out of reach of many people. Blessed with taste buds that react to the grape rather than hops or malt, wine-drinkers have really only three alternatives. One is to buy the cherished bottle on fewer occasions and to eventually stop buying the wine altogether. The second is to win the football pools, throw this book away and immediately order two or three hectolitres of 1er cru 1976 Château Mouton-Rothschild or whatever. And the third and certainly the most practical is to make wine at home.

'This fine magnum of 1959 Lafite . . . I am bid £1000 . . .'

'. . . going . . .'

'. . . . gone!'

Wine and fruit growing areas in the world

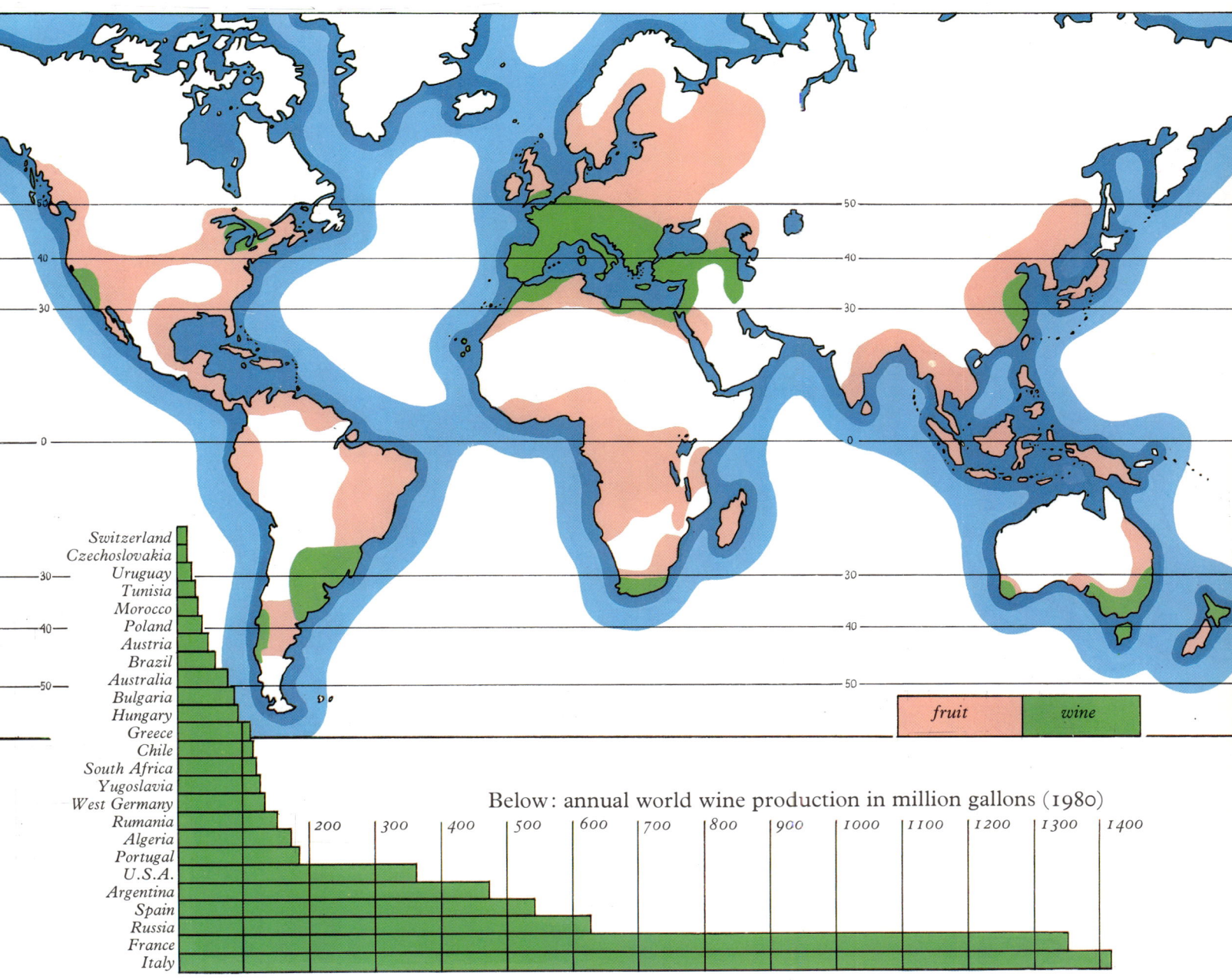

fruit | wine

Below: annual world wine production in million gallons (1980)

Switzerland
Czechoslovakia
Uruguay
Tunisia
Morocco
Poland
Austria
Brazil
Australia
Bulgaria
Hungary
Greece
Chile
South Africa
Yugoslavia
West Germany
Rumania
Algeria
Portugal
U.S.A.
Argentina
Spain
Russia
France
Italy

200 | 300 | 400 | 500 | 600 | 700 | 800 | 900 | 1000 | 1100 | 1200 | 1300 | 1400

The advantages of making wine at home

Home-made wines once had a country-cousin aura of mead, cowslip and berries about them; sweet and sticky liquids that were reverently taken out of dark cupboards in old farmhouses. They were fermented with baker's or brewer's yeasts or with so-called 'wild' yeasts which, if they did not spoil the wine altogether, achieved an alcohol content that was far too low to give it good keeping qualities.

Today's home-winemaker is more fortunate than his predecessors because a prospering home-wine industry is eager to supply everything he can possibly need. Even grapes come in cans in the form of concentrated grape juice, and a wide variety of specially cultured yeasts help him to produce the kind of wine he wants. There is also an extensive range of low-priced equipment designed to fit the small space available in the modern home.

What, then, does home-made wine cost? A standard 75 cl bottle of quality wine can be made at home for as little as 60p – in the shops a bottle of grape wine of similar quality may cost up to ten times as much. This of course excludes the initial outlay on equipment and basic ingredients but this is minimal and they will last for many years. The basic equipment will allow you to make 13 litres (3 gal) of wine every year, and for the price of another storage vessel, you have the capacity for fermenting a further 4 litres. Home-made wines really do mean that the occasional dinner party creates no financial upheaval!

Since the ingredients are chosen and controlled by the winemaker, wine made at home is as wholesome as any commercial wine – sometimes a good deal more so. Making wine is an adventure and the fact that no wine can ever be repeated exactly, however precisely the ingredients are put together again, adds to the excitement. New wines are always different from past vintages and you will often be surprised by subtle changes of taste or a sudden leap in quality. As you become more experienced at winemaking, your palate will become more discerning. Wine has to be tasted in its early stages as well as when it is maturing so anyone who takes up the hobby will find himself recognising an increasing number of significant tastes and developing a greater general understanding of wines.

Winemaking can be a social activity too – winemakers' clubs are springing up in many areas, where enthusiasts come together and exchange news, recipes and sometimes equipment.

Winemaking is a leisurely business. A period of sudden activity may be followed by many weeks or months when nothing happens. Patience is essential to let the wines mature – it is quite possible to make a drinkable wine in six months; but it will taste bland or rough and have little character. Wine that is to satisfy a critical palate has to be given time. The first year can be particularly irksome because there is as yet no proof that the whole effort was worthwhile. Now and then you probably take a sip of the new vintage and – the nature

of wine being what it is – you probably find it tastes dreadful. But don't despair: young Sauternes and young clarets often taste extremely rough and may reek of drains or worse. Only when the next season arrives and you begin to wonder if it is worth making yet another evil-tasting pool of wine, will last year's vintage have had time to mature a little. Then is the time to open a bottle, let it breathe for a few hours, taste it and . . . Eureka! Somehow it has become wine and it tastes good!

Winemaking and the Law
In Britain, no restrictions are imposed on making wine at home as long as it is for private and social consumption. No duty is required to be paid on it *as long as it is not being sold*. Duty is payable, however, if it is offered at parties where admission is charged or included in raffles, bazaars and auctions, even if they are organised for a charity or other good cause. Neither can homemade wine be given away if there is an implied advantage in doing so, for instance, if you wanted to promote your business or restaurant by offering free wine with a meal.

Laws relating to wine do differ, however, not only between countries but also sometimes within national boundaries – historic principalities and islands in particular may have different charters, so if you live outside the United Kingdom it would be as well to check up on the local situation.

Unlicenced home *distilling* on the other hand, is illegal in Britain and most other countries. This is the process by which wine is heated in a still and the resulting alcoholic vapour led to a condenser where it cools and forms a spirit that is higher in alcohol content than the original liquid. The cycle may be repeated a few times, each distillation producing a stronger spirit, but when not expertly done, this can be dangerous since unacceptably large amounts of fusel oil and methyl alcohol may be created. These are poisons and can kill.

Separating water from alcohol through *freezing* is another method of strengthening a wine's alcohol content, but the home winemaker should not attempt this either as the health risks (not to mention the legal risk) are far too great.

The basic winemaking method

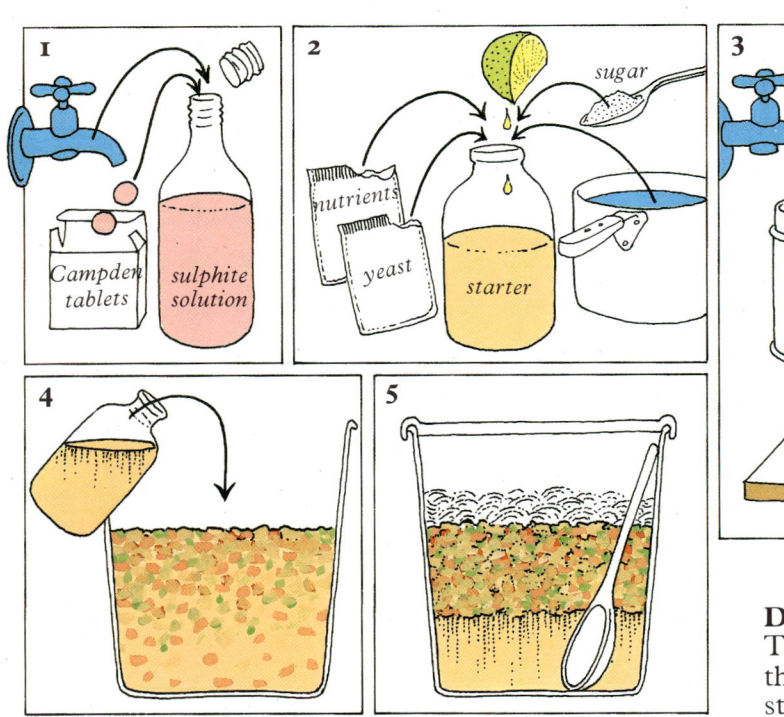

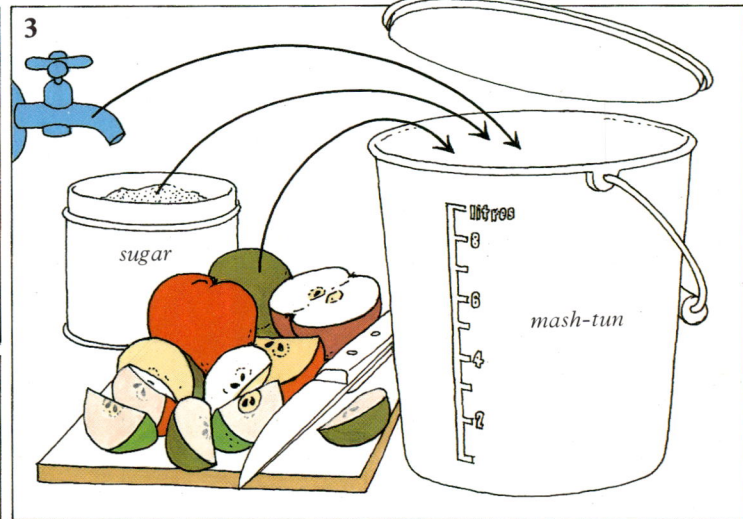

The process of making wine is always the same; once yeast, sugar and water are placed together in a vessel, the liquid or 'must' begins to ferment. Since such a mixture would produce a rather tasteless liquid, fruit, berries or flowers are included at the same time to give it flavour, body and aroma. At the end of the fermentation, the wine yeast has converted virtually all the sugar into alcohol.

Winemaking always follows the same pattern, so to familiarise the reader with the steps that need to be carried out they are set out day by day below. When later on you make your first wine by following one of the recipes, it is a good idea to keep your own diary as you go along, recording and dating the various stages as you complete them.

Day 1
This is the busiest day, when three jobs need to be done: the first is the preparation of a sulphite solution and the sterilising of all the equipment and the working surfaces (see page 26). Then a 'yeast starter' is made up to activate the yeast (see page 41) and it is left in a warm place. Lastly, in a plastic bucket with lid (the mash-tun), the fruit juice or fruit pulp is combined with water and sugar to form the must. The liquid should fill no more than three quarters of the mash-tun as the must will later bubble up.

Day 2
The now active yeast starter is added to the must and to prevent a cap of pulp forming on its surface, the must is stirred three times daily. This is best done with a sterilised plastic spoon which can then remain inside the closed mash-tun. Over the next few days, the 'initial' or tumultuous period, the must ferments vigorously and may froth.

Day 6

A glass fermenting vessel (either the demijohn or a similar container), a plastic strainer and a funnel are sterilised in the same way as the mash-tun. The must is slowly strained into the fermenting vessel and the residue lightly pressed until most of the liquid has passed through the strainer. The liquid level should rise no higher than the shoulder of the fermenter to allow for the frothing action of the yeast. A sterilised rubber bung and airlock are then inserted into the mouth of the fermenter.

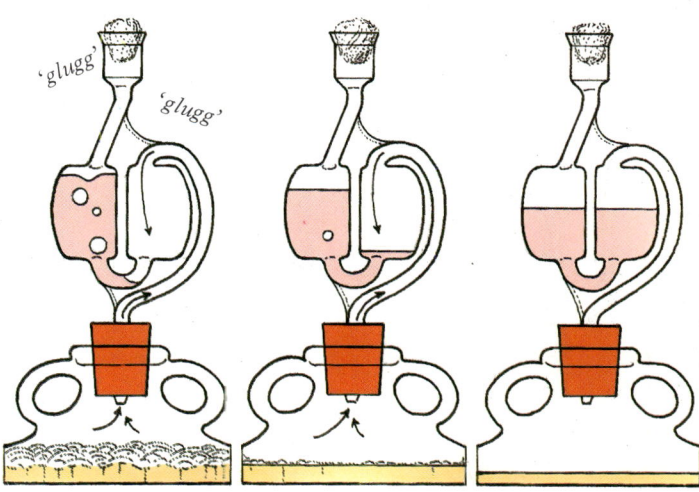

'glugg' 'glugg'

Day 6 onwards

From now on, the fermentation is 'slow' – it proceeds calmly. It is enjoyable to watch the action in the airlock, since every time a bubble of carbon dioxide is given off, an equal weight of alcohol has been produced by the yeast cells. At first, a bubble appears almost every second, but after a week or so the rate slows down until towards the end of the fermentation there may only be a bubble once every minute. As the yeast produces more and more alcohol, the liquid in which it finds itself becomes increasingly hostile to its existence. The yeast colony dwindles and sediment from the fruit and dead yeast cells forms a thick layer on the bottom.

15

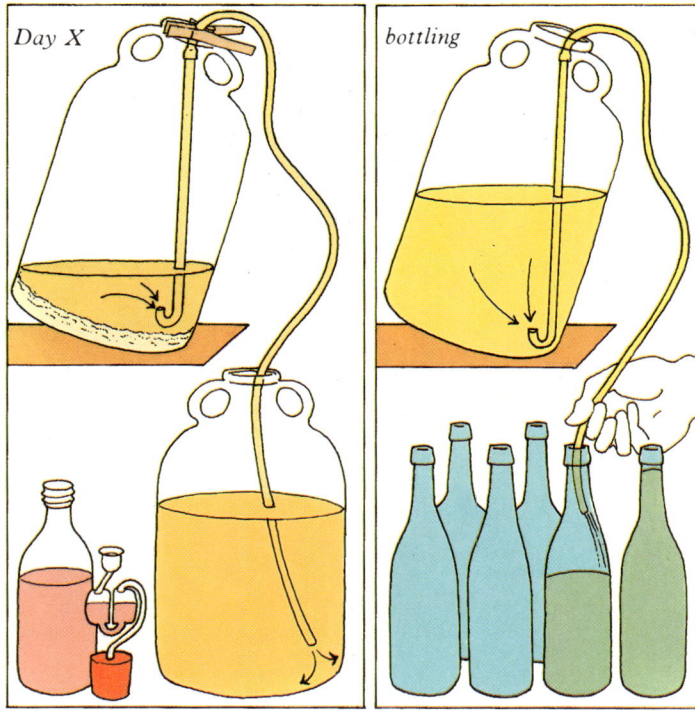

Day X

bottling

Day X

'Racking' is a medieval-sounding term for the simple task of transferring the fermented must from one vessel to another with a syphon, leaving the sediment or lees behind. Racking helps to clear a wine. It is not possible to specify a date for racking, since some fruit wines may have ceased to ferment after two weeks, while others may require two months or more. When no more bubbles appear in the airlock, fermentation is over and the wine must be racked.

Syphoning is done with a 1 m (3 ft) long flexible plastic tube to which a rigid section is attached as shown. The fermenter should be placed well above the mash-tun for the syphoning action to commence. A clothes peg will prevent the intake of the syphon from touching the lees. When the fermenter is nearly empty, it is tilted gently to collect any remaining clear liquid.

The now empty fermenter is washed out with fairly hot water to remove the lees. In a final operation, the young wine is poured back from the mash-tun into the fermenter which now becomes a storage vessel and the airlock is replaced. Most winemakers have more than one vessel, which allows them to rack the wine straight into a storage vessel without having to use the mash-tun.

Day Y

Within a few weeks, the wine will be really clear and must be racked for the second time. It will also need to be topped up to just under the rubber bung. With the airlock still in place, the wine is then stored away from strong light or with the vessel covered with a dark cloth.

Maturing

Maturing is the period during which wines not only clear and become bright but in which they also continually improve in taste and bouquet. Great wines result from a perfect choice of ingredients but they need particular attention and care when they are stored in bulk. The time needed for maturing differs and while some white wines are ready for drinking within twelve months, red wines should be stored for at least three years.

All maturing wines should be kept in a cool and dark place and need to be racked every two months during the summer and every three months during the winter. They will still contain a few yeast cells, which slowly settle as sediment and have to be removed. Regular racking is also essential to prevent re-fermentation when the warmer weather returns. If wines are bottled too early, the bottles may burst under pressure, which can be both messy and dangerous.

Bottling

Again, wine bottles, corks or stoppers and the syphon have to be sterilised. The wine is then at last syphoned from the storage vessel into one bottle after another. The bottles are finally corked or stoppered, labelled and stored in a dark place at about 10°C (50°F). White wines can be drunk after a minimum of three months, but red wines should be left to improve for a further year in their bottles.

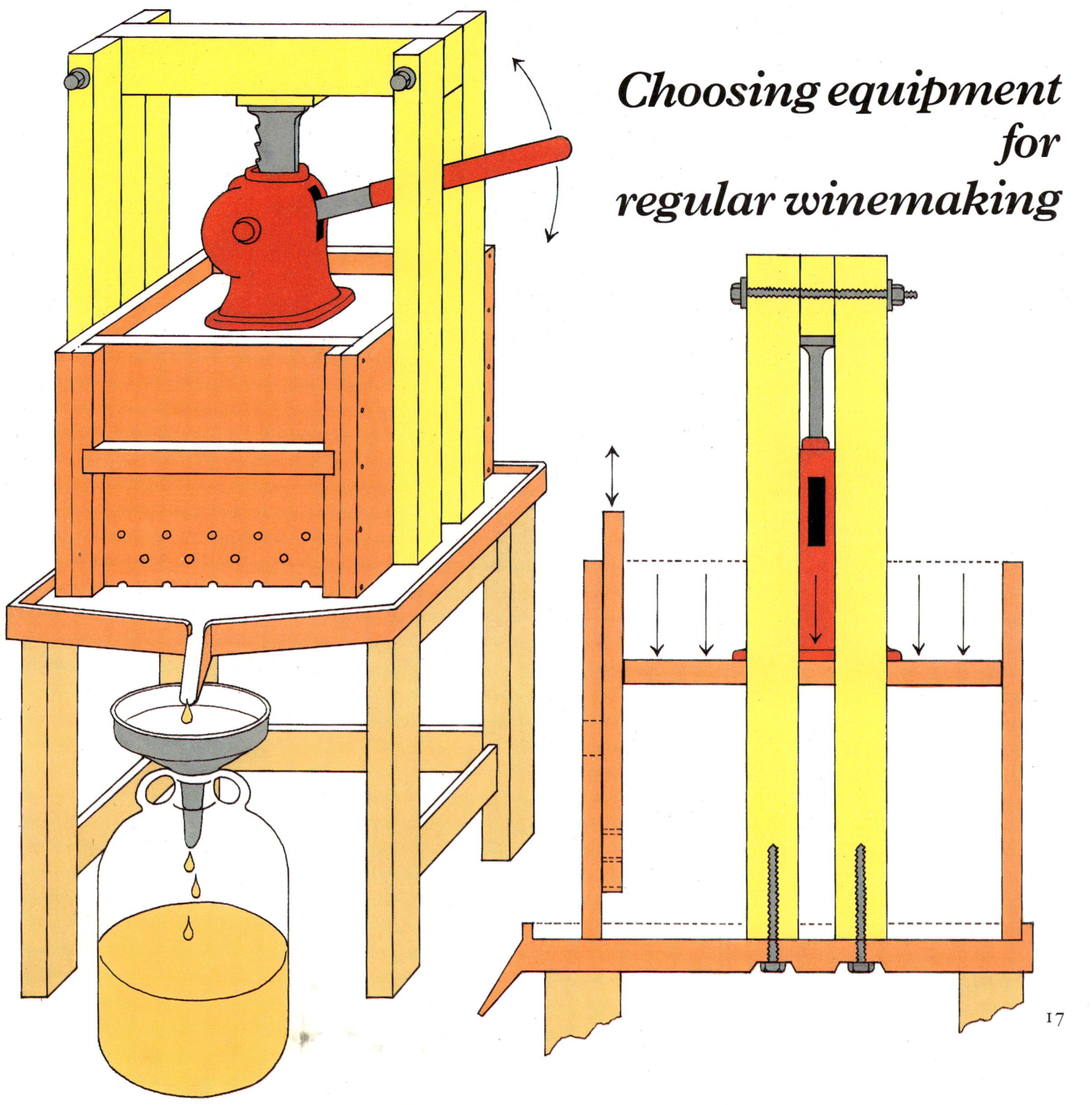

Winemaking equipment consists mainly of storage vessels which are bulky, heavy when full and often fragile. Utensils with which to prepare the must and measure liquids have to be durable and easy to clean, but some materials are more suitable than others.

Metals

Copper, zinc, brass, iron (even chipped enamel ware), lead, tin, galvanised or soldered ware should never be allowed to come into contact with acid fruit juices, even for short periods. The acids in fruit or wine quickly dissolve tiny amounts of these metals which then remain in the wine as a metallic haze and spoil it. Lead is particularly dangerous as it can actually render a wine poisonous.

Stainless steel, aluminium and sound enamel ware are more acid-resistant and can therefore be employed for a short time, such as when cutting, crushing or boiling fruit, but they are also unsuitable for longer fermenting or storing periods.

Glass

Glass is one of the best materials to use in winemaking. It is chemically inert, easily cleaned and relatively cheap and since containers made of it are transparent the wine can be inspected. The major drawback is its fragility, and large 25–50 litre (5–10 gal) vessels have to be protected by wicker, wire or wooden cages to prevent accidents. Apart from clear glass containers, dark-coloured ones are useful for maturing red wines as their opacity prevents light from reaching the wine – strong light would bleach its colour and even ruin it if the exposure were prolonged. Clear glass vessels can be made opaque by painting on the outside or simply by covering them with a dark cloth.

Apart from standard 'demijohns' and 'carboys', the larger champagne bottles make excellent fermenting vessels. Do bear in mind that you'll need at least two identical vessels – the second one for racking.

Demijohn	4.5	litres	1	gallon
Carboy	14	litres	3	gallons
Carboy	22	litres	5	gallons
Rehoboam	4.5	litres	1	gallon
Methusalah	6	litres	$1\frac{1}{3}$	gallons
Salmanazar	9	litres	2	gallons
Balthazar	12	litres	$2\frac{2}{3}$	gallons
Nebuchadnezzar	15	litres	$3\frac{1}{3}$	gallons

A bottle brush is an essential piece of equipment since its flexible handle allows you to reach awkward corners. It is often used to remove the hardened film on the bottom of a vessel which is caused by the minerals in a must.

Bottles, corks and labels

Only true wine bottles stand up to the pressure that may sometimes build up through a secondary fermentation. Never use screw-top bottles which may explode and cause serious damage. Bottles of green or brown glass give some protection against the effects of light but add the odd clear bottle per batch so that you can inspect the condition of the wine.

The cylindrical cork is the traditional means of sealing a bottle of wine, but with the disadvantage that it requires to be driven flush home, for which some type of corking machine will be needed. The simplest corking device is the 'Corker' and when you use it, hold the bottle in your other hand covered with a thick cloth in case of a possible breakage. Never use corks that have been pierced by a corkscrew since bacteria will find a way into the wine – new corks from a wine-shop are not expensive and are safer.

Tapered corks do not fit wine bottles well (they are often pushed out again), but large tapered corks are useful for sealing all kinds of fermenting and storage vessels as well as casks.

Cork stoppers with a flange made of a plastic material are a second choice but can serve if they are tied down with string and finally covered with a capsule made of foil or plastic. Stoppers are often forced out again by the pressure built up when driving them in: put a length of thin string into the bottle first, then press the stopper in and hold it down. When the string is pulled out, the compressed air will escape with it.

The most popular and practical stoppers are made of polythene and are available from many suppliers. They ensure a close fit and being plastic, need only be sterilized for an hour or so. Plastic stoppers can be used over and over again.

Tin-foil capsules are simply pulled over the cork or stoppered bottle-top and then squeezed by hand. Plastic capsules are peeled off a backing sheet and will then adhere firmly with their sticky inner surface. Both types of capsule are an extra defence for the wine against possible infection, and will also inhibit any leaking or 'weeping'. If there is a choice, use red or black capsules for red wines, and green, yellow or white ones for white wines so that they can be identified in a bottle rack.

Because it will be impossible after some time to remember what wine a bottle contains, bottles need to be labelled in some way. As will be explained later, a consecutive numbering system is the simplest method of identifying the fermenters and if you have to bottle a large volume of wine, each bottle from one fermenter could be given the same number. Simply place a little stick-on label with the number high on the shoulder of the bottle so that it can easily be seen when stacked in a bottle rack.

More elaborate labels are useful if you want to bring out a bottle for a special occasion or make a present of it to somebody. Suppliers have many types of label in stock and decorative wine labels on gummed paper can be made at home – see illustration. Labels should display the year when the wine was made (the vintage), the type of wine it is – for example, 'Rose Petal Wine' – and your name and/or address. Place the label as shown, making sure that it is centred between the two mould seams of the bottle.

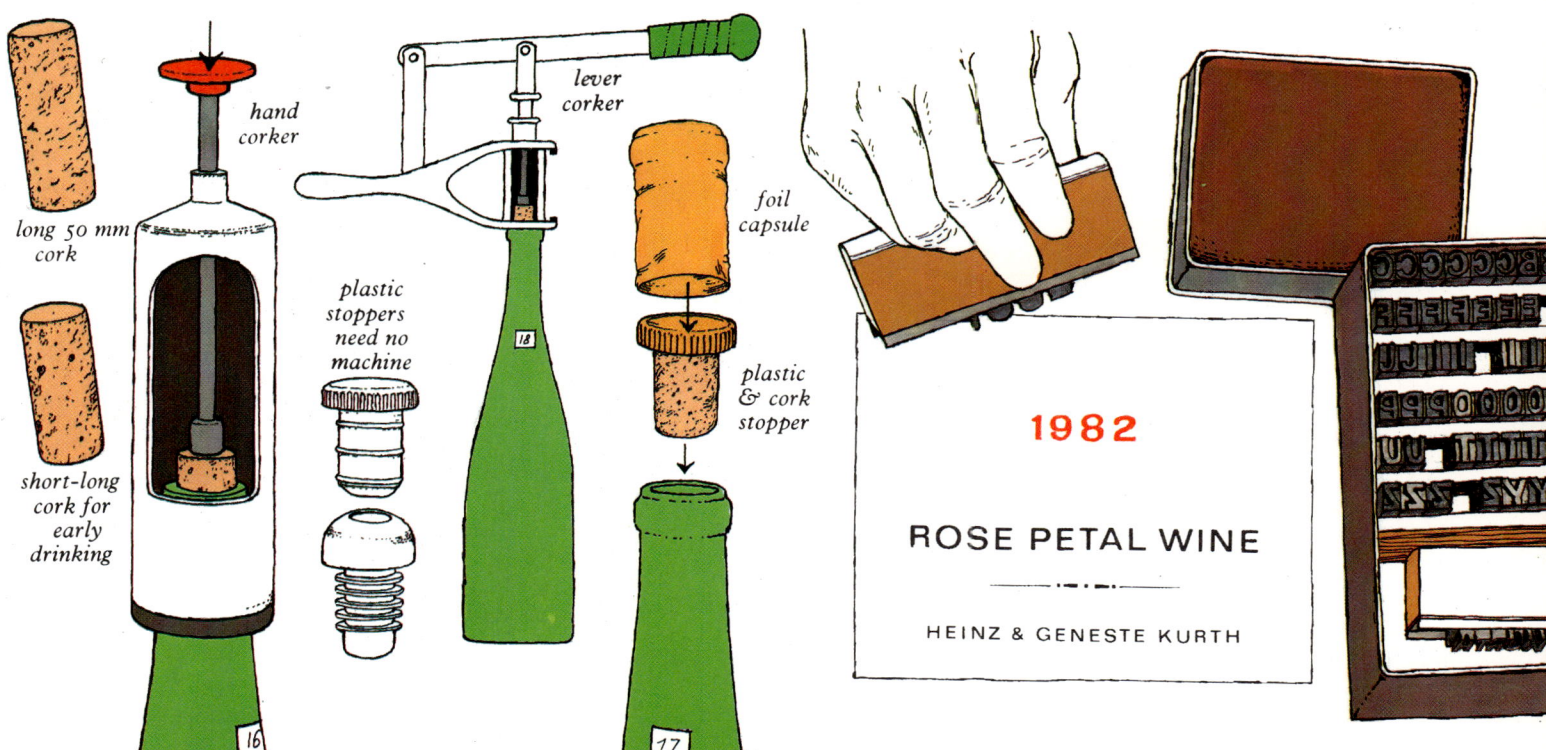

long 50 mm cork

short-long cork for early drinking

hand corker

plastic stoppers need no machine

lever corker

foil capsule

plastic & cork stopper

1982

ROSE PETAL WINE

HEINZ & GENESTE KURTH

Plastics

Most winemaking equipment is also available in plastic which is easy to clean, light in weight and much less likely to break than most rigid materials. Some plastic containers, however, are semi-rigid or even collapsible, in which case they need support in the form of a box made of cardboard or wood.

Clear or white nylon, terylene, PVC, polypropylene and polyethylene are all suitable as long as no plasticiser, which would leach out and contaminate the wine, has been incorporated during manufacture. Coloured bins or buckets, not originally intended for food, may be toxic and should be discarded for the same reason. If you have to use one, line it first with a bag of limp, transparent polythene. So, before buying any plastic container, make sure it is of a grade approved for food use and the tougher and whiter it is, the better.

When being given or offered secondhand vessels, reject any which may have been contaminated by previous contents. The odours of many chemicals, vinegar, oil and petrol are retained within a plastic material, cannot be removed and would consequently contaminate any wine. This property of retaining or even transmitting smells is a disadvantage common to all plastics. For instance, if you employ plastic vessels for the storage of wine, do not store paraffin or toxic substances in the vicinity as smells and fumes will be transmitted from one vessel to another.

Large polypropylene vessels are the best for the initial stages of fermenting; they are often supplied with a graduated scale of litres/gallons which is very helpful when the proportions of a fresh must have to be calculated. Another important feature is the lid, which should fit tightly but open and close easily, since musts have to be stirred at least three times a day. Many winemakers also use these vessels for fermentation and the maturing of wines, in which case the lid has to have an opening designed to take an airlock. If you have to store must in a cool place, vessels complete with built-in heaters, separate immersion heaters or warming pads are also available – they have,

of course, to be fitted with a thermostat to avoid overheating.

Clear plastics such as polythene are ideal for small pieces of equipment: airlocks, measures, hydrometers, stoppers and syphons – they are easy to keep clean, do not break with normal usage and are generally very cheap.

For the crushing, mincing or pressing of fruit, metal would be the best material since it has tensile strength but iron or steel cannot be used on its own due to the danger of acid corrosion. Metal that is covered with a plastic compound does not have this disadvantage and a number of plastic-coated mincers, crushers and presses are now on the market.

Bags made of linen or cheesecloth are invaluable for the pressing of pulp to extract juice, but fine mesh nylon bags are the best – their fibres do not absorb the liquid and need to be cleaned less often during pressing.

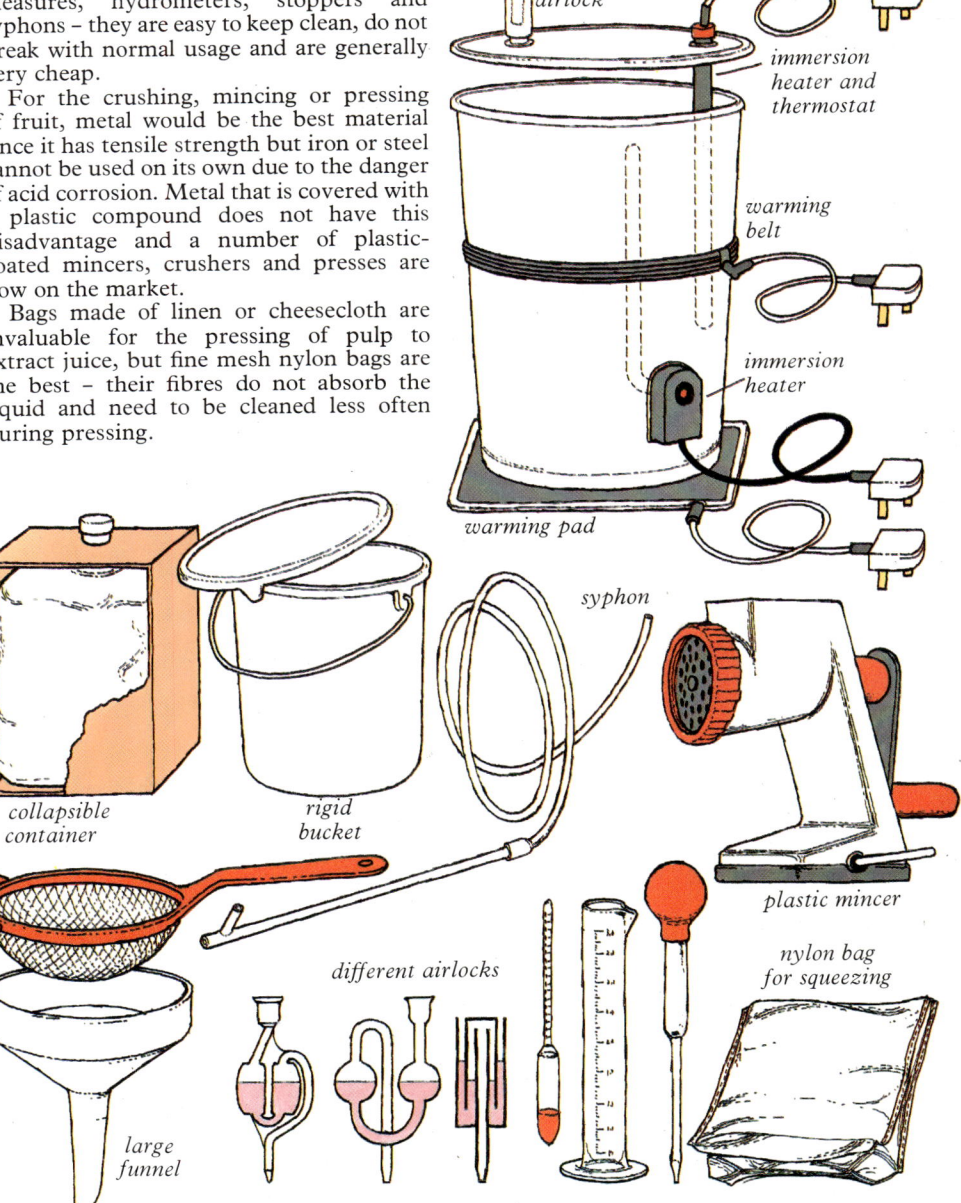

Alternative methods to keep the contents of a 25 litre rigid plastic fermenter warm.

airlock

immersion heater and thermostat

warming belt

immersion heater

warming pad

syphon

collapsible container

rigid bucket

plastic mincer

nylon bag for squeezing

different airlocks

large funnel

Wood

Oak is the traditional material used by winemakers all over the world. It is employed for fermenting and storage vessels as well as for the presses used to extract juice from grapes or fruit. The beginner in winemaking and the amateur who wants to limit his output to mainly white wines can do well without oak casks which need to be large and are therefore heavy and expensive, take up much space and are the very devil to clean and to handle.

Again, when buying or being offered secondhand casks, make sure that they have contained nothing but wine, cider, port or beer. Casks or barrels are essential for the maturing of red wines, which need continuous access to small amounts of oxygen from the air; the microscopic spaces between the wood fibres allow such a transit free of dust and bacteria. Since the ratio of transmission is lower in large casks and higher in small ones compared with the volume of liquid, the smallest practicable size holds about 40 litres (9 gal); if smaller casks are employed, the storage period must be reduced to a few months instead of years to prevent the wine from over-oxidising – three months in wood, followed by three months in glass and so on.

Pin	20 litres	4 gallons
Six	27 litres	6 gallons
Firkin	40 litres	9 gallons
Kilderkin	81 litres	18 gallons
Hekto	100 litres	22 gallons
Barrel	162 litres	36 gallons

To avoid any possibility of contamination, a new cask has to be conditioned for wine storage – an arduous routine which, fortunately, need only be carried out once:

1) Fill the cask with water and keep topping it up for a day or two so that the staves expand and are watertight.

2) Empty the cask and fill it with hot water in which washing soda has been dissolved (1 kilo for every 20 litres of water). Leave for 24 hours, then pour off. Repeat the process for a second-hand cask that is in poor condition.

3) Rinse with cold water to remove the soda.

4) Fill the cask with hot water and let it stand for 24 hours. This is to bleach out any remaining soda and tannin from the staves. Pour the water away and repeat until the poured-out water is clear and shows only a pale, tea-coloured tint. Finally rinse and drain.

5) Fill the cask to about $\frac{1}{8}$th of its volume with sulphite solution, close the bung hole and roll the cask for half an hour over the ground. Every now and then stand the cask on each end to ensure that the head-staves are also sterilised.

6) Discard the sulphite, rinse and drain at least twice with water to wash out any trace that remains.

7) Add 1 teaspoon each of citric acid and grape tannin to a bottle of your worst wine and pour it into the cask. Close the bung hole and roll the cask again for half an hour.

8) Much of the wine, tannin and acid will have been absorbed by the wood; pour out the rest and discard. Your cask is now ready and should be filled at once.

Fill the cask with a fermenting must first since this helps to condition the wood more quickly. After fermenting, the cask need only be rinsed to remove the lees from the must; but it is vital to fill the cask at once with a new must or a new wine so that it does not dry out.

Never stand casks on end for any length of time because the upper end piece will dry out and eventually leak. And, if a filled cask were left to just lie upon the ground, it would soon spring a stave and leak from then on. A cask should be supported either on a wooden cradle or on four pieces of shaped wood with the bung hole uppermost.

Taps, too, can give trouble – they often leak where tap and taphole join because the wood of the tap dries and shrinks. Much wine can be lost in this way. Either plug the taphole with a fitted piece of oak or buy casks without a taphole, checking and racking the wine through the bung hole.

If these precautions are taken, and the hoops painted regularly to prevent rusting, oak casks should last almost indefinitely.

bung

hoop

stave

stave

cradle

Wood is also used in the manufacture of fruit presses and small models have been specially designed for the amateur. Unfortunately they are costly and the d.i.y. man will find it cheaper to make his own, perhaps using a car-jack for the mechanical part (see page 17). While oak and other hardwoods are still the best material for this, waterproof plywood, particularly birch-ply, will readily stand up to repeated soaking.

If you are planning an annual output of more than, say, 65 bottles, a wooden bottle-drying rack will save much time when washing and sulphiting wine bottles – see illustration.

Earthenware

As in ancient times, large crocks made from this material are very useful storage vessels: they are easily kept clean and, being opaque, are particularly useful for maturing red wines. They are also heavy, break easily and, unless inherited or given, are expensive. It is important to check the type of glazing employed: modern earthenware is usually salt-glazed and perfectly safe but older vessels, especially those of oriental origin, were often lead-glazed, which would poison any wine stored in them. As a rough test, see whether the glaze is applied as a thin and clear film and if it echoes with a sharp 'ping' when tapped, it has a salt-glaze.

If the glaze has been applied in a thick, opaque or syrup-coloured film which can be dented with your fingernail and gives a dull sound when tapped, it is likely to be a lead glaze.

small grape or fruit press

home-made bottle-draining rack

fruit crusher made of oak

various 15-60 litre clay jars

The amount of wine you can make obviously depends on the time you are willing to spend on the process and the space you can spare for the storage of maturing wines. You can decide upon the scale of your planning and choose the right equipment for your particular requirements, using the examples below.

Throughout this book, the basic quantity of wines made is 4.5 litres (1 gal) which is the standard volume of the ordinary demijohn. Of course, if you want to use a larger or smaller fermenting vessel, all you have to do is measure its capacity and adjust the ingredients accordingly, except the yeast, since the same amount will ferment anything between 4 and 20 litres (1–5 gal). Do not, however, make a quantity of wine smaller than, say, 4 litres since a small volume of liquid is liable to change its temperature too often (between day and night or with the central heating switched on or off) and this will adversely affect the fermentation process.

The demijohn winery

Anyone with limited space and time, wishing to make wine without much upheaval can, by working a total of 3–4 days over the year, produce 48 bottles of wine in two bottling sessions. An extra 4.5 litre (1 gal) storage vessel increases the capacity of his winery by another 12 bottles. Equipment can be stored on a couple of shelves in or near the kitchen with the fermenters standing on warming pads or being placed in an airing cupboard for the duration of the fermentation. One vessel should always be kept empty to receive the contents of the first full fermenter when the wine is being racked.

The carboy winery

The more ambitious winemaker will probably buy large quantities of local fruit cheaply in bulk. Alternatively, many cider farms are glad to sell pressed fruit juice at little cost. 100 kilos of fruit will produce many 22 litre (5 gal) musts for white wine and the same musts, with a few kilos of elderberries added to them, make an exquisite rosé. The time required for these activities would be a 'wine-holiday' of some 8 days for preparing the musts, plus another 5 days or so spread over the year for racking and bottling.

A separate area, perhaps a small basement room, would be an ideal place for the winery where equipment as well as storage vessels and bottles can find a place. A sink with running water would help greatly but if there is none, the musts could be prepared in the kitchen and the fermenting mash-tun carried to the winery. Four 45 litre (10 gal) carboys, plus the extra one needed for racking, will finish a minimum of 250 bottles of wine per year.

The self-sufficient winery

If your house is surrounded by a garden, you could be living in a winemaker's paradise. A large garden with a number of fruit trees and, ideally, one elder will provide most of the fruit for winemaking. Even a small garden will produce fruit and berries from shrubs as well as parsnips and, of course, roses. Other ingredients can often be obtained from neighbours in exchange for a bottle or two of your wine.

Musts will probably have to be prepared in the kitchen because of the requirements of cleanliness, but fermentation can take place in a conservatory or an outhouse where low-power immersion heaters could provide the necessary warmth. You also have the opportunity to install a few casks there in which to mature red wines.

Time will have to be spent on the garden itself, of course, but the time actually devoted to winemaking over the year is similar to that required for the carboy winery and will result in at least 300 bottles of wine every year.

Preparing the must

Guarding against bacteria

Wine not only delights the human palate, it is also very attractive to a large army of marauding micro-organisms, particularly in the early stages. A square centimetre of the surface of a ripe fruit has been found to contain up to 150,000 fungus spores and bacteria, many of which are carried to it by the air or by attaching themselves to the feet of insects. *Drosophila melanogaster*, the fruit fly, carries a particularly vicious bacteria which, if it were to reach any must or wine, would cause it to become vinegar. That is why sterile cleanliness is of such importance in winemaking and any methods used should ensure that only one type of organism – the yeast fungus – is allowed to do its work in the must.

Since wine is a food, only two means can be employed by the amateur to protect it: sterilisation by heat (boil-

ing will kill bacteria, though the must may be re-infected on cooling), or longer-lasting protection by the gas sulphur dioxide which is given off by burning sulphur or emitted from a solution of potassium metabisulphite or sodium metabisulphite, known as sulphite. Sulphite can be bought in the form of Campden tablets, each of which contains 0.44 g of sulphite.

Equipment that is going to come into contact with a must or with wine must be washed in hot soapy water, then rinsed with tapwater and given a final wipe or rinse with the sulphite solution. The standard concentration is 2 sulphite tablets to 0.5 litre (1 pint) of water and this concentrated solution should be kept in a stoppered bottle. Large vessels and fruit presses can be wiped with a cloth soaked in the solution.

The musts themselves are sterilised initially either by boiling for a short time or by pouring boiling water over the ingredients. Alternatively, and more effectively, cold musts can be sterilised with 2 crushed sulphite tablets per 4.5 litres (1 gal) or 3 tablets during hot weather. If you use this method, wait for 24 hours before introducing the yeast, by which time the effect of the sulphite will have worn off.

Insects are attracted to the open ends of airlocks and sometimes drown in and contaminate the water. To keep the water sterile, drop $\frac{1}{16}$ sulphite tablet into the water seal. After a few weeks the water (and the sulphite) should be renewed, and the opening of the lock closed with a plug of cotton wool.

Other defence barriers are created by the wine itself. As fermentation gets under way, the carbon dioxide produced by the yeast fills the unoccupied space in the fermenter and forms a protective blanket over the must. Later, when more than 10% of alcohol has been produced, the liquid becomes inhospitable for many though not all types of spoilage organism: this is the original reason why export wines such as Madeira and Port were fortified with brandy, so that the higher alcohol content made them safer in transit and subsequent handling.

Empty jars and bottles remain sterile if 10 mm ($\frac{1}{2}$ in) of sulphite solution is left in them and the tops are sealed.

Sulphite is also an effective agent for the preservation of finished wines. It is therefore a good idea to add $\frac{1}{2}$ tablet for the third and subsequent racking (see page 44). But when you want to make a sweet wine, add 2 sulphite tablets at the first racking because it will stop the action of the yeast.

Adding the water

More than 80% of the volume of wine is made up by water and, fortunately, this ingredient presents few problems. Whereas a special water quality is essential for the distillation of whisky, hard or soft water does not seem to make any difference to the taste of finished wines. A few winemakers who live in hard-water areas boil all the water they use, which precipitates some of the calcium carbonate and dissolves any chlorine gas that may have been added to the public water system as a disinfectant. Boiling, however, also expels oxygen which the yeast needs, and whenever the home winemaker uses boiled water, it should be stirred vigorously first to aerate it and so replenish the oxygen.

Plain tap water often contains minerals which are beneficial to yeast activity and so does spring water. Well-water and rainwater on the other hand may contain sulphuric impurities from the air and should only be used after filtering through a chamois cloth and thorough boiling. With these last two exceptions, water with which to prepare *cold* musts needs no boiling. Simply add tap water to the other ingredients, and two or three sulphite tablets per 4.5 litres (1 gal) will sterilise both the water and the ingredients (see page 35).

Water that is to be added to an already fermenting must or to finished wines needs to be both sterile *and* cool and there are two simple ways of achieving this. One method is to boil as much as you need and let it cool to 24°C (75°F) or less. The other method is to fill the largest clean vessel you can spare with tap water, sterilise it with two sulphite tablets per 4.5 litres (1 gal) and seal it with cotton wool. The water will be ready for use 24 hours later.

The role of sugar in the must

After water, the most important ingredient in the must is sugar, which the yeast converts into ethyl alcohol and carbon dioxide in approximately equal proportions. Ordinary white, granulated household sugar from sugar cane or beet is used by most winemakers because it has no effect on either the flavour or the colour of the wine. Brown sugar, golden syrup or treacle may be useful for after dinner wines where their brown colour is not obtrusive and the caramel taste does not impair the flavour.

Sugar, or sucrose, is a disaccharide which is first *inverted* by the yeast into glucose and fructose (both are monosaccharides). A few winemakers use invert sugars to shorten the period before fermentation begins but invert sugars are usually much more expensive than ordinary white sugar and they do not seem to hasten the onset of fermentation very much. Grape concentrates, raisins and honey are a source of invert sugar but their real advantage is elsewhere: they contribute floral esters, and therefore bouquet, as well as vinosity to a wine.

Clover, acacia and heather honeys are very acceptable sugar substitutes, but not eucalyptus honey as this imparts an unpleasant flavour. Liquid or crystalline honeys should be stirred into an equal quantity of water and then boiled for a few minutes since they are not free from bacteria.

Sultanas and raisins are dried grapes which are usually covered with a thin film of paraffin as a protection against infection. For winemaking this film has to be removed by washing them in warm water in a colander prior to slicing or mincing.

Canned grape concentrates usually need to be diluted with water in the proportion stated on the can in which they are bought. Many recipes at the end of this book include quantities of undiluted grape concentrate and if you plan to make several different types of wine in one session, it is cheaper to buy large cans and draw from them the required quantities. Select the cheapest brand on the market for your first wines, only buying special concentrates such as 'Hock' or 'Burgundy' when you are confident that the extra expense is justified.

Before adding granulated sugar to a must, it is better to dissolve it in hot water first so that it becomes a syrup. Undissolved sugar would settle at the bottom of the vessel in a compact layer – far too high a concentration for the yeast surrounding it. The yeast would consequently cease to be active or even die and the fermentation would 'stick'. A stuck fermentation is one where the yeast has become inactive far ahead of the planned termination of the process, and the result is an over-sweet wine.

It is also sometimes possible to add the sugar directly when the must is being prepared. Boiling water is poured over the sugar and some of the other ingredients and the must stirred until all the sugar has dissolved, sterilising the must at the same time.

Since the amount of sugar in a must determines the maximum amount of alcohol the wine will have, a useful fact to remember is that when converted, 450 g (1 lb) of household sugar will result in approximately 5% alcohol in 4.5 litres (1 gal) of must. This formula will help you to make the type of wine you want:

1. kilo (2¼ lb) sugar in 4.5 litres (1 gal) of must produces dry wine with about 12% alcohol.
1.35 kilos (3 lb) sugar in 4.5 litres (1 gal) of must produces a medium wine with about 15% alcohol.
1.6 kilos (3½ lb) sugar in 4.5 litres (1 gal) of must produces strong/sweet wine with about 17% alcohol.

The formula applies, of course, to the total sugar that is in the must including any natural sugar which may be present in the fruit itself. While this has been allowed for in the recipes, only a hydrometer can help you to find how much sugar there is in fruit (see page 30).

Alcohol-seeking optimists may well assume that the more sugar that is added to a must, the stronger the wine will become. This is quite correct in theory but unfortunately there is a limit to the amount of alcohol that the yeast can survive in without poisoning itself – and be assured that the authors have tried hard to find out what that limit is!

The answer is that 15% to 18% alcohol is as much as the yeast cells can tolerate: when that limit has been reached, the cells begin to die. They sink to the bottom of the vessel and the fermentation is finished.

Sugar-feeding

Most wine yeasts will ferment musts containing up to 1.25 kilos (2½ lb) sugar per 4.5 litre (1 gal) without any trouble and up to this amount of sugar can therefore be included at the outset. Musts that are intended to yield more alcohol (for after dinner wines for example) need to have the sugar added in stages. 'Sugar-feeding' avoids causing a shock to the yeast cells which, when suddenly surrounded by a strong sugar solution, may become dehydrated and cease to function.

If a recipe calls for more than 1.25 kilos (2½ lb) of sugar, do not add it all at once but begin the ferment with only 1 kilo (2 lb) and add the remainder in quantities of 110 g (4 oz) each time the fermentation has slowed down. To add the sugar, put it into a large (sterilised) jug and pour 0.5 litre (1 pt) or so of the fermenting must onto it. Then, without heating, stir the solution with a clean spoon until all the sugar has dissolved and return the enriched must to the fermenter. To obtain the highest possible alcohol content, such as that required for vermouth or port-type wines, this process is best conducted with the help of a hydrometer (see following pages).

110 g sugar

adding about one litre of fermenting wine to the sugar

the sugar may take 10 minutes to dissolve

returning the enriched wine to the fermenter

sulphite

Controlling the fermentation with a hydrometer

While all the wines at the end of this book can be made without a hydrometer, using one allows the fermentation to be more carefully controlled and can help to pinpoint trouble, thereby ultimately contributing to the making of better wines.

The hydrometer is a very simple device for measuring the density of a liquid – in other words it tells the winemaker how much sugar there is in his must. By taking a second reading after fermentation, when the sugar has been converted, he can compute the amount of alcohol that has been produced. Inexpensive plastic models are now available which are less fragile than glass models and it is a good idea also to obtain a tall, slim jar in which the hydrometer can float. This will also serve as a container when the hydrometer is not in use, and if the jar is calibrated in millilitres, it will allow small volumes of liquid to be measured accurately.

All measuring scales have a zero point and the hydrometer's zero point is 1000 – the density of pure water. This is a useful indicator for verifying the accuracy of a new instrument or checking its soundness after it has perhaps been dropped accidentally: simply fill the jar with water and if the reading is 1000, the hydrometer is in order.

If you then fill the jar with a liquid such as wine, which contains alcohol, the hydrometer sinks to quite a depth in it. This is because alcohol is volatile, and less dense than water. Conversely, the instrument will be pushed high up if the jar is filled with a liquid such as a sugar solution that is denser than water. The graduated scale on the stem allows the density or 'specific gravity' (SG) of the liquid to be read off at the point where the stem rises from the surface.

For winemaking, a hydrometer calibrated from about 980 to 1170 will cover most needs although later on, for greater precision, you may want to use two instruments, one reading perhaps 950–1100, the other 1100–1200, which provide greater stem-length and therefore a clearer and more accurate scale. How can readings be lower than zero which is 1000? Pure alcohol has a specific gravity of 794 and any presence of it in water must give a reading lower than 1000.

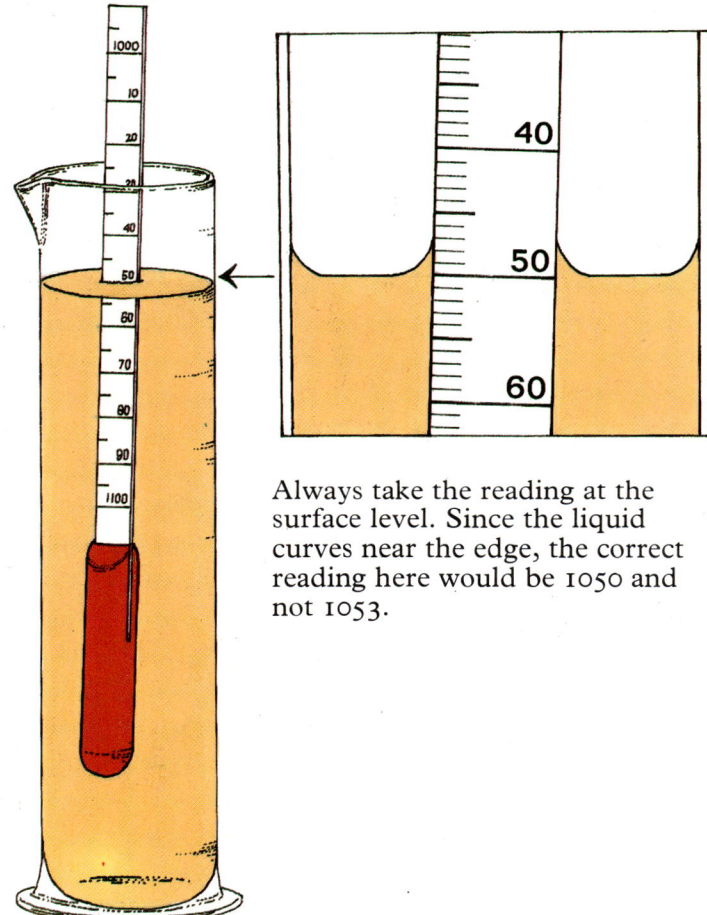

Always take the reading at the surface level. Since the liquid curves near the edge, the correct reading here would be 1050 and not 1053.

Some types of hydrometer are not calibrated in degrees of specific gravity but give 'sugar content' and 'potential alcohol'. While these are the vital elements, it is better to become familiar at the start of the hobby with the specific gravity scale. The table printed here and repeated at the back of the book allows degrees to be converted into sugar content or sugar into alcohol content.

Note that any liquids that are to be measured should be near room temperature – about 15°C (60°F) – otherwise the following small corrections will need to be made:

Temp. of liquid	correction	as applied to SG
5°C	−2	998
10	−1	999
15	none	1000
20	+1	1001
25	+2	1002
30	+3	1003

When you are making wine by sugar-feeding, it is often simpler to take a first reading of the must to establish the natural sugar content, then add the required sugar and ferment to the desired gravity, noting down only the final reading. The total alcohol can be computed simply from the table. For instance:

Sugar in the must	450 g (1 lb)	
Sugar added	1125 g (2½ lb)	

Total sugar	1575 g (3½ lb) = potential alcohol:	21%
Less final reading of say, 1015:		2.1%

Alcohol content of wine:	18.9%

Two difficulties affect the otherwise straightforward hydrometer procedure. One is the quantity of un-dissolved solids in 'thick' musts and the other the volume of the sugar itself.

Musts that are to be fermented on the pulp contain, besides sugar, a large amount of suspended plant matter – the pulp – as well as acids, salts and pectins, all of which increase the specific gravity. So if a very accurate reading is required, a small sample of the must has to be strained through a fine cloth and allowed to settle before the specific gravity is measured. Another method gives a useful but slightly less accurate result: simply strain a portion of the must into the hydrometer jar, measure its specific gravity and subtract between 6 and 10 points from your reading (1020-1024 instead of 1030 for instance): this should be a sufficient allowance for the suspended plant matter.

The other difficulty is that sugar also has volume and the space it occupies has to be allowed for. When sugar is added to a must, it will increase the volume and paradoxically dilute the must at the same time. That is why it is a good idea always to keep musts below their final volume.

Gravity table

spec. grav. (S.G.)	potential alcohol in % volume	weight of sugar		
		grammes per litre	grammes per gallon	per gal lb / oz
1000	0	0	0	0 0
1005	0.7	12	56	0 2
1010	1.4	25	112	0 4
1015	2.1	38	171	0 6
1020	2.8	51	229	0 8
1025	3.5	63	283	0 10
1030	4.2	76	342	0 12
1035	4.9	88	396	0 14
1040	5.6	101	454	1 0
1045	6.3	112	504	1 2
1050	7.0	128	570	1 4
1055	7.7	139	626	1 6
1060	8.4	152	684	1 8
1065	9.1	164	738	1 10
1070	9.8	177	796	1 12
1075	10.5	190	848	1 14
1080	11.2	203	913	2 0
1085	11.9	215	968	2 2
1090	12.6	228	1026	2 4
1095	13.3	240	1080	2 6
1100	14.0	253	1138	2 8
1105	14.7	265	1192	2 10
1110	15.4	278	1251	2 12
1115	16.1	290	1310	2 14
1120	16.8	303	1363	3 0
1125	17.5	315	1417	3 3
1130	18.2	326	1470	3 5
1135	18.9	341	1534	3 7
1140	19.6	354	1593	3 9
1145	20.3	366	1650	3 11
1150	21.0	379	1704	3 13

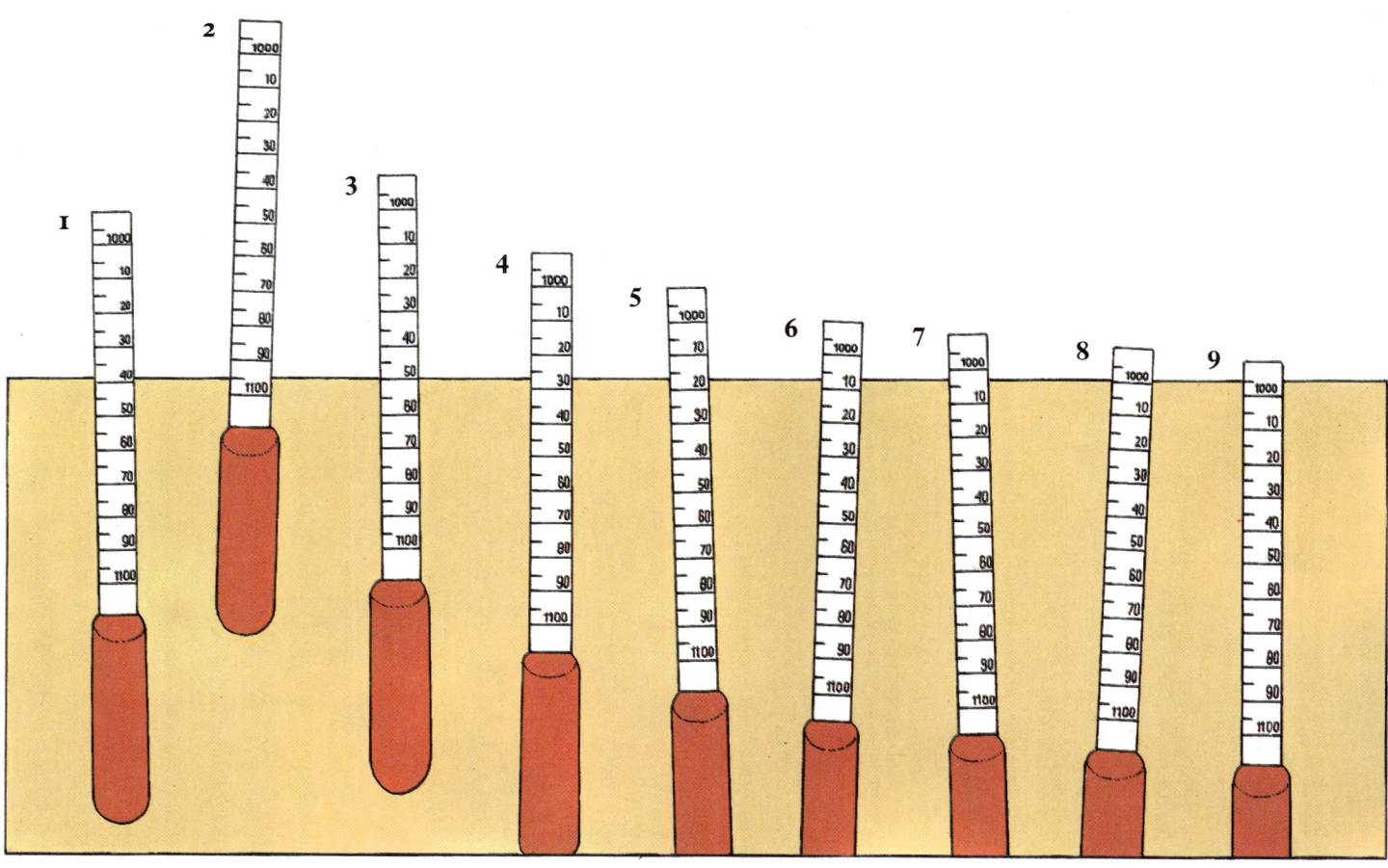

1 This is how the hydrometer helps you to find the natural sugar content of the must. Before any sugar is added, clean the hydrometer and jar in hot water or the sulphite solution and fill it with a sample of the must. Lower the hydrometer into the liquid and swirl the stem a few times to free any clinging air bubbles, which would tend to lift the instrument slightly and produce a false reading. If the reading is, say, 1040, by looking at the table you will find that the fruit juice has a natural sugar content equivalent to 450 g (1 lb). If you wish to make 4.5 litres (1 gal) of a *dry* wine (which would need 1.2 kilos (2½ lb) of sugar in all), the conclusion is that you need to add only another 670 g (1½ lb) of household sugar.

2 Add the required sugar to the must and take another reading. Note it down on your data sheet, since it will later help you to predict the amount of alcohol your wine will have. Say the reading is now 1095.

3–8 There is no need to take any readings during the fermentation but if you did, each day you would find the hydrometer positioned lower in the liquid; quite noticeably at first and less so towards the end of the fermentation.

9 The hydrometer is now very low (and the airlock has ceased to bubble), both indicating that the end of the fermentation is near. You can now calculate how much sugar is remaining: if the reading is around 1005, your wine will have some sugar left and will be slightly sweet and if that is what you want, stop the ferment by racking and adding 2 crushed sulphite tablets. But if you prefer a drier wine, continue fermenting until the reading drops to around 995. How strong is the wine? By consulting your data sheet you see that the original reading was 1095 and that your last reading was 995 which is a 'gravity drop' of 100. From the table you will see that a drop of 100 is equivalent to 14% of alcohol.

Controlling acidity

All musts should contain a number of organic plant acids. Without these, they do not ferment well and the wine cannot develop a pleasant flavour. It may acquire a medicinal taste and be infected more easily, which means it will not keep. Three acids in particular are vital in winemaking, and they are dominant in particular fruits: tartaric acid (in grapes), malic acid (in apples) and citric acid (in lemons). A combination of all three is beneficial to most wines. Malic acid in a wine leads sometimes to a second 'malolactic' fermentation during which the sharp-tasting malic acid is converted by members of the lactobacillus into the milder and more pleasant tasting lactic acid.

It is almost impossible to tell the acid level of a sample of fruit by just tasting it. Its stage of ripeness, the mineral content of the ground on which it grew and the length and quality of the season all influence acid levels – sometimes drastically. While the recipes at the end of the book are as balanced as possible, exceptionally bad or good seasons and early or late picking do affect the acidity of the fruit and therefore of the must. Nevertheless, when the must is prepared, its acid content should be increased by 1 tsp per 4.5 litres (1 gallon) where the table shows a low acid content and by $\frac{1}{2}$ tsp where it shows a medium one. This is for light table wines but the amounts should be doubled for apéritif and after-dinner wines.

If the principal acid of the fruit is malic, for instance, make up an acid mixture from equal portions of tartaric and citric but where the acid content is shown as 'low', make up the extra acid from equal proportions of all three acids.

Acids can be bought as crystals (which have first to be dissolved in hot water) or in the form of powder which can be added directly to the must. They work out cheaper if bought in bulk and will last for many years if they are kept in airtight containers. Since acids have such a great effect on the taste of any wine, many winemakers check every must first with an acid-testing 'titration' kit. Very accurate but inexpensive outfits are obtainable: the instructions that come with them may differ from one make to another but most of them measure the volume of a neutralising agent needed to react with a sample of the must. After some calculations, the answer is supplied in parts per thousand, or ppt.

Dry wines generally have an acidity of 3.5 to 4.5 ppt while sweet wines need between 4.5 and 5.5 ppt to counterbalance the taste of their higher sugar content. Full-bodied red wines, particularly those that are to

ingredient	principal acid	average acid content
apples	malic	medium
apricots	malic	medium
bananas	citric	low
bilberries	citric	high
blackberries	malic	high
cherries	malic	high
crab apples	malic	high
currants	citric	medium
damsons	malic	medium
dates	none	none
dried fruit	malic	none to low
elderberries	citric	low
flowers, fresh	none	none
flowers, dried	none	none
gooseberries	malic	high
grapefruit	citric	high
grapes	tartaric	medium
grape concentrate	tartaric	low
greengages	malic	medium
herbs	none	none
loganberries	citric	high
lemons	citric	high
oranges	citric	high
peaches	malic	medium
pears	citric	low
plums	malic	high
raisins	tartaric	low
raspberries	citric	high
rhubarb	oxalic	high
root vegetables	none	none
sloes	malic	high
strawberries	citric	high
sultanas	tartaric	low

mature for four years or more need between 6 and 7 ppt. One level 5 ml teaspoon of powdered acid will raise the acidity of 4.5 litres (1 gallon) by about 2 ppt.

Over-acidity can be a problem too. It is sometimes caused by using too much fruit in the must so that a sharp-tasting wine is produced. There are preparations on the market, such as powdered chalk, which lower the acidity, but since these substances remove other valuable elements as well, they are better left alone. The simplest cure for over-acidity is to dilute the must by increasing its volume. Water and extra sugar (in the basic proportion) have to be added, so producing perhaps twice the volume of a milder wine. There is another alternative, which is to do nothing about the over-acidity. Bottle the wine and later on when the occasional over-sweet, bland or flat-tasting batch needs to be improved, blending it with the more acid wine will improve it (see blending, page 50).

Tannin from teapot or phial

The effect of tannin is easily confused with that of acid since both give 'zest' or 'bite' to wine. The bitterness of tannin is usually noticed in the front part of the mouth, on the sides of the tongue and the inside cheeks, while acid is tasted at the back of the mouth or sensed behind the front teeth.

Red wines may have four times as much tannin as white wines because they are pulp-fermented; a process which not only takes colouring matter but also tannin from skins and stalks. This is why red wines need to mature longer – they need time to loose their initial bitterness but will in the end become superior to whites. A small excess of tannin helps to clear musts more rapidly, reduces hazes and increases the keeping property of a wine. During maturing, the small excess is gradually reduced, but if a wine has too great an excess of tannin, it can be reduced through fining (see page 46).

Fruit, berries and flowers vary in their tannin content and when using fruit high in tannin, the winemaker should be cautious and not exceed the stated fruit content. Conversely, he should provide extra tannin for fruit that is deficient in it.

Unfortunately, no simple test for tannin can be undertaken by the amateur. His only guide is to check the fruit to be used against the list set out below or to taste the wine and remedy any shortcoming as soon as the fermentation is over. Grape tannin, for example, is a powder extracted from grape pips and grape skins that can be bought at most winemaking suppliers. Simply add 1 tsp to musts made from fruit listed below in paragraph 3 and $\frac{1}{2}$ tsp to musts listed in paragraph 2.

---

1) elderberries, sultanas, bilberries, currants, grapes, sloes and raisins contain sufficient tannin (elderberries in particular have an excess of it), so do not exceed the amounts stated in the recipes.

2) apples, apricots, bananas (with skins), black-currants, bilberries, peaches, and sloes will supply just enough tannin of their own if they are pulp fermented. For juice fermentation, add half the tannin needed for ingredients under 3).

3) bananas, cereals, dates, figs, flowers, herbs, pears, prunes, and vegetables are deficient in tannin and need to have some added.

Tea is another very convenient source for tannin although since the degree of infusion cannot be controlled precisely, the tannin it supplies will vary. It is at least worthwhile for that reason to establish a set routine when brewing it, using perhaps 2 heaped tsps per 0.25 litres ($\frac{1}{2}$ pt) of boiling water and letting it infuse until cooled to 22°C (70°F). The tea is then strained onto 4.5 litres (1 gal) of must.

Blending the must

Blending is a word which some traditional winemakers seldom use, their being of the opinion that a wine should be made from only one ingredient so that it can justly be described as apple wine, elderberry wine and so on. But there are many other winemakers who consider the quality of a finished wine of greater importance than its ancestry and who say that no single type of fruit other than the grape can really produce a superior wine; quite apart from the difficulty of obtaining well-ripened and fresh fruit every time. They also point out that professional vintners not only blend different types of grape but also make up a lack of sugar, a deficiency in colouring matter or over-acidity after a short or rainy season by sugaring or blending.

Both arguments have some justification but the authors offer a third suggestion, which is to prepare musts from a single type of fruit, flower or berry as a *main ingredient*, but to add to them small amounts of other ingredients to make up any deficiency. Wines made from flowers on their own, for instance, lack body so bananas, raisins and acids really have to be added to remedy this shortcoming, while apple wines would taste harsh without the addition of raisins or grape concentrate to give them vinosity.

Blending can take place either at the beginning of the winemaking process, by selecting suitable ingredients for a must, or by blending finished wines as explained on page 50.

While the recipes at the end of this book have already been balanced, blending with different ingredients can result in many hundreds of different tastes and you will eventually want to experiment with your own recipes.

Extracting flavour

WARNING: a great number of plants contain harmful substances, some of which can cause death while others could make you very ill. The following list shows ones to avoid but it is by no means complete and it would be as well for anyone without special training to use only plants mentioned in this book for winemaking.

Poisonous: aconite, alder, azalea, baneberry, belladonna, berberis, black nightshade, bluebell, buttercup, clematis, cowbane, cyclamen, daffodil, deadly nightshade, foxglove, fungi, hemlock, honeysuckle, iris, ivy, laburnum, laurel, lilac, lobelia, lupin, narcissus, poppy, rhododendron, rhubarb leaves, sweet pea, wood anemone, yew.

Harmful or unpleasant flavours: agrimony, borage, broom, cabbage, carnation, chrysanthemum, clover, coconut, jasmine, lettuce, marrow, orchids, pinks, pumpkin, tomato, tomato stems, tulip, turnip.

While water, sugar and the yeast provide the framework for a wine, it is fruit that gives it flavour. As in the production of grape wines, there are basically two ways of making fruit release its flavour – *juice fermentation* and *pulp fermentation*. Either of these methods can be used for most ingredients but juice fermentation will usually produce better light and delicate white wines while pulp fermentation is more suitable for medium and sweet white wines and full-bodied red wines. The method employed may also be governed by the equipment available and by the nature of the fruit that is to be included: grapes and oranges, for instance, give up their juice easily while fruits such as berries or plums need to be pulp fermented since the juice contained is closely interlocked with fine and pulpy flesh and pressing the fruit would only result in a thick puree.

Juice fermentation
The must may be fruit juice or grape concentrate that has come straight from a can or it may be juice obtained by hand, with an extractor, with a fruit press or through boiling. The juice is usually diluted with water to avoid too harsh a flavour or too much acidity (see recipes). It is then sulphited – 2 tablets per 4.5 litres (1 gal) and syphoned after 24 hours, leaving most of the pulp behind. Grape concentrates have no pulp.

35

A *fruit crusher* is useful for breaking up the fruit prior to pressing. A is a small, hand-operated type made from aluminium and B has a larger capacity. A very handy and cheap model consists simply of a stainless steel rod with a masher at its working end – C. It is driven by a power tool as shown and needs a lid fitted with a hole to prevent splashing. The resulting pulp is then pressed by hand or in a fruit press.

Pressing by hand is the simplest method, although the pressing of quantities of fruit for more than about 14 litres (3 gal) of must may become strenuous. First break the skin of grapes, plums or peaches with your hands, remove the larger stones and drop the pulp into the mash-tun, adding 2 sulphite tablets per 4.5 litres (1 gal). Add cold water to make up 75% of the final volume and stir the must repeatedly. Scoop some of the must into a fine-mesh nylon bag and press with both hands until most of the juice has come out. Discard the pulp. Continue until all of the must is free of pulp then cover the must with a lid. Next day, carefully syphon the must into the fermenter, discarding any further sediment. After sugar has been added, the must is ready for the yeast.

Fruit juice can be produced cold in a *blender* D or with the help of steam in a *juice extractor* E and each type deals with batches of about 2.5 kilos (5 lbs) of fruit at a time, ejecting juice and pulp separately. Apples need to be washed and quartered first and in the case of the cold extraction a certain amount of water has to be added to every batch so that the milling can proceed smoothly. Water for this is best poured from a measuring jar so that its volume is known and can be allowed for.

A *fruit press* is essential for the extraction of fruit juice in bulk. Apart from home-made models (see page 17), there are presses of different capacity, design and, of course, price on the market. The basket of the press is filled with pulped, crushed or sliced fruit and as the screw is gradually tightened, a close-fitting head piece is forced down, squeezing the juice out of the fruit. After sulphiting, the juice is allowed to settle overnight and syphoned the next day.

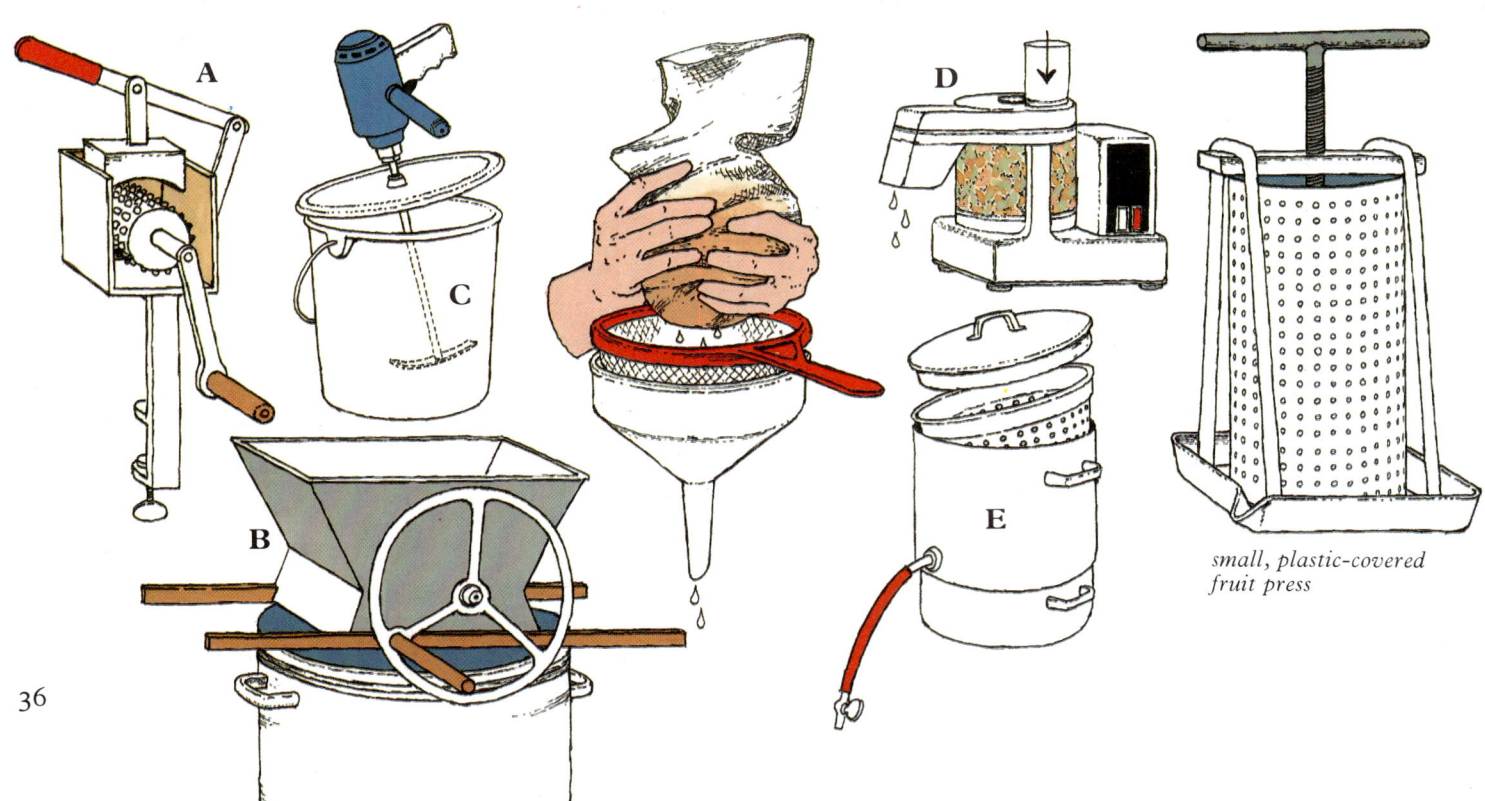

small, plastic-covered fruit press

fruit	preparation apart from washing and cutting out rotting parts :	juice fermentation :		pulp fermentation :	
		cold-pressing	boiling	cold-sulphited	boiled water over must
apples	crushed or sliced	best	no	yes	no
apricots	stoned	best	no	yes	no
bananas	sliced	no	best	no	no
berries	squashed	yes	no	best	no
cherries	crushed	no	no	best	no
currants (red/white)	crushed	yes	no	best	no
damsons	stoned	no	no	best	yes
dates, dried	crushed or minced	no	no	best	yes
elderberries	crushed or milled	yes	no	best	yes
flowers	petals only	no	no	best	no
grapefruit	halved and squeezed	best	no	some peel	no
grapes, white	crushed	best	no	yes	no
grapes, red	crushed	yes	no	best	no
grape concentrate	open can and dilute	best	no	yes	no
gooseberries	crushed	no	no	best	yes
greengages	stoned	no	no	best	yes
herbs	leaves only	no	no	best	yes
loganberries	crushed	yes	no	best	yes
lemons	halved and squeezed	best	no	yes	no
melons	peeled and crushed	yes	no	best	yes
oranges	halved and squeezed	best	no	yes	no
plums	stoned	no	no	best	yes
peaches	stoned	best	no	yes	no
pears	crushed or sliced	best	no	no	no
raisins	minced or sliced	no	no	yes	best
rhubarb	sliced and crushed	best	no	no	no
raspberries	crushed	yes	no	best	yes
root vegetables	sliced	no	best	no	no
strawberries	crushed	yes	no	best	yes
sultanas and other dried fruit i.e.					
apricots	minced	no	no	best	yes
sloes	stoned	no	no	best	yes

Boiling in water is the only way to extract juice from bananas, parsnips or other root vegetables, but boiling should always be kept to a minimum since otherwise large quantities of pectin and starch are released, which causes haze (see page 38). Use only the clear and strained juice after boiling and discard the pulp without straining or pressing it.

Pulp fermentation

This is sometimes the only technique possible for obtaining flavour from berries, plums or dried fruit. The fruit has first to be crushed, pounded or minced so that the skins are broken to allow the yeast to reach the flesh of the fruit.

The must intended for pulp fermentation can be sterilised either with boiling water or with sulphite tablets. Add to the pulp all, or a portion of the sugar, pour over it boiling water constituting up to 4/5th of the final volume and stir until the sugar has dissolved. Add any acids at this stage since they help to invert the sugar. Then let the must cool to less than 22°C (70°F) before adding the yeast.

Alternatively, add cold water and sterilise the pulp with two sulphite tablets per 4.5 litres (1 gal) – three tablets in hot weather, and close the lid. Make up the yeast starter, but do not add the yeast until 24 hours later when the effect of the sulphite has worn off as otherwise it would be inhibited.

While the thickish pulp ferments during the first fermentation period, fruit flavour as well as colouring matter leaches out into the must. After 3 to 7 days (see recipes), the pulp can be pressed – the yeast will have weakened the fabric of the fruit so that it gives up its juice more easily. Place the funnel and the strainer over the fermenter, scoop some must into the fine-mesh nylon bag and press slowly, until almost all the juice has run into the fermenter. Repeat until the mash-tun is empty. Discard the pulp, except in the case of elderberries which can be re-soaked and pressed at least twice more to yield additional juice.

Avoiding trouble from pectin and starch
Most wine disorders become apparent only after the wine has been racked, when it may well be too late for any remedies. But the major trouble caused by excess pectin, and the lesser one caused by the presence of starch can be avoided by treating the must *before* fermentation.

The fleshy part of most fruits and vegetables contains starch and other gelatinous carbohydrates, commonly called pectins, which have colloidal properties – that is, they gel. This is useful for making jellies and jams which have to set, but even minimal pectin traces may cloud a finished wine and such a haze may be difficult to clear later. That is why boiling should be kept to a minimum or avoided whenever possible because boiling releases larger amounts of pectin than cold preparation.

To ensure that the wine will be clear when finished, *all* musts should be treated as a matter of routine with a pectin-destroying enzyme such as Pectozyme or Pectinol to break down the long molecular pectin chains into shorter, non-colloidal units. Pectic enzymes are bought in powder form and, unless the packet states otherwise, one heaped teaspoon is sufficient to clear 2.5 litres (5 pts) of juice or pulp.

Starch may similarly cause haze, especially in wines made from roots or unripe fruit, and a standard remedy is to treat such musts with another enzyme: Amylozyme 100 or Amylase 2209 ($\frac{1}{2}$ tsp to 2.5 litres – 5 pts of must) to lessen any risk to the finished wine.

Enzymes are sensitive organic substances – they become inoperative when exposed to heat, so never add them to hot musts but wait until the temperature has dropped to 24°C (75°F) or less. They can be added to cold musts at once, even before the yeast, since they will not be affected by sulphiting. Enzymes and yeast function happily side by side throughout the fermentation.

A bouquet of flowers, herbs and spices
Even perfectly flavoured fruit wines often fail to communicate their quality to the nose – they lack bouquet. Bouquet is formed by some acids, notably succinic acid which, while the wine matures, produces fragrant and volatile esters, detectable as a pleasant aroma. Unfortunately, few fruits match the bouquet of a wine made from fully ripened grapes: if the fruit is fresh and ripe, a little aroma will be present but unripe, badly stored or refrigerated fruit will have none.

Many winemakers, therefore, add a small quantity of flower petals to almost every wine they make. Used in small amounts, flowers do not affect the flavour of a wine and as well as giving it aroma they can also add colour. Flowers are best gathered on a sunny warm day when the petals are full of natural oils, undiluted by outside moisture.

Elderflowers are best taken from the type of tree that has white (and fewer) rather than creamy (and many) blossoms. Discard any green parts (the stem, leaf and calix) to avoid a bitter taste and use the petals quickly, before they have lost their aroma. Elderflowers have a strong and heady perfume and 0.25 to 0.5 litres, ($\frac{1}{2}$ to $\frac{3}{4}$ pint) per 4.5 litres (1 gal) is sufficient for most wines. If more flowers are added, the wine develops an unpleasant 'catty' bouquet. Dried elderflowers are equivalent to four times the weight of fresh ones, usually 14 g ($\frac{1}{2}$ oz) per 4.5 litres (1 gal) and can be bought at most supply shops throughout the year.

Rose petals are a useful alternative to elderflowers, with the advantage that they are in bloom for a longer time. White and yellow petals should, of course, be added to white wines, but a mixture of white and red petals will give a white wine a pleasant hint of rosé and exclusively red petals will enrich and deepen the colour of red wines. Normally 150 ml ($\frac{1}{4}$ pint) of strongly scented or up to 400 ml ($\frac{3}{4}$ pint) of weakly scented petals are enough for 4.5 litres (1 gal) of must.

A mixture of elderflowers and roses produces the finest bouquet while mayblossom, cowslip and primrose petals can be used as a second choice.

Flowers should be added to a must some 8 or 10 days *after* the start of the slow fermentation period so that their volatile perfume is not driven out either through any initial heat treatment of the must, or through the strong carbon-dioxide emission in the early and more vigorous stage of the slow fermentation.

Gather the flowers on the day you want to use them. Remove any green material and place the petals in the measuring jar – do not press them down. Then soak them in a weak sulphite solution of $\frac{1}{2}$ tablet per 0.5 litres (1 pint), drain and shake them hard in a strainer. Open the airlock of the fermenter and feed the petals into the must. Leave them in the must for the duration of the ferment and strain them out at the next racking.

Herbs and spices. While flowers improve the bouquet of a wine, the flavour of many apéritif and after-dinner wines, which are high in alcohol, can be strengthened or made spicier by the inclusion of a small quantity of herbs or spices.

Depending on whether they are added to a light, strong, sweet or dry wine, herbs and spices produce many different flavours and it is not possible to describe the many variations that can be obtained.

56 g (2 oz) of fresh or 28 g (1 oz) of dried herbs will flavour a wine noticeably. The herbs can be boiled for 20 minutes and strained before use, be added directly to a must or added (sulphited and shaken-out) after fermenting. In the last instance, they can be added at any time between two rackings. If you are at all uncertain about the degree of flavouring that is taking place, pack the herbs in a muslin bag and suspend it in the fermenter, checking the taste of the wine from time to time.

Wines can of course also be made entirely from herbs as the main ingredient (see recipe section).

Winemakers with a sweet tooth may like to try the very potent artificial flavour essences sold by chemists. Before a whole gallon is put at risk, however, an eye dropper should be used to test a cherry, raspberry or sherry flavour in a single glass of a finished wine; after which the required amount for the whole quantity can be measured out.

Compiling practical data sheets
Whatever ingredients you use in a new wine, be sure to keep a record not only of the quantities involved but also of the method used to extract the flavour (boiling, cold must etc.). Such a record will be invaluable when you are enjoying the new wine a year later and want to recall how it was made.

A set of data sheets should be kept in a file and, if you use a hydrometer, note on the sheet the various readings of specific gravity to compute the alcohol content of the wine. Number each data sheet consecutively, and use the same number to label your fermenters as well as the finished bottles, which saves you the trouble of having to write all the particulars on every label.

16	*Cherry Wine*
Ingred.:	*3½ kg mixed cherries, 900 g sultanas, 300 g sugar 1 teasp. acids and Burgundy yeast.*
July 25	*Yeast starter. Cherries and sultanas pulped, 2 sulphite.*
July 26	*Combined in mash-tun with enzyme, total sugar and yeast starter. Reading 1080.*
Aug 3	*Into fermenter. Reading 1030.*
Aug 30	*Fermentation ceased. Reading 1000. Racked.*
Sept 25	*Wine clear. Racked and ½ sulphite.*
Dec 26	*Racked and ½ sulphite.*
Mar 25	*Racked and ½ sulphite.*
May 25	*Racked and bottled.*
Nov 30	*Taste: fruity with some bouquet. Too young for drinking. 12% alcohol.*

Fermenting the must

Yeast strain	approx. max. alcohol tolerance in % by volume	colour (rosé can be made with any):	body:
all purpose	15	red and white	light or medium
Beaujolais	14	red	light
Bordeaux (Claret)	16	red and white	medium
Burgundy	15	red	medium
Chablis	15	white	medium
Champagne	14	white	light
Graves	15	white	medium
Hock (many varieties)	12	white	light
Madeira	18	red and white	strong
Pommard	15	red	medium
Sauternes	16	white	strong
Super, all purpose	18	red and white	strong
Tokay	18	white	strong

Choosing the right yeast

Yeast is a living colony of microscopic, single-celled fungi, which, given the right living conditions, and the right food, multiply and go to work converting sugar to alcohol.

Wine yeasts (*Saccharomyces ellipsoideus*) can be bought as Hock, Burgundy, Sauternes, Pommard, Tokay yeast and so on; they are yeasts that have been taken from the area in which these famous commercial wines are produced and have been cultured in laboratories. They are sold in liquid form (which is the most vigorous but also short-lived) or as granules (which will last for up to two seasons), either in jars or in small packets. A small packet or teaspoon of yeast will normally be enough to activate a yeast starter and the yeast starter will easily inoculate 4–20 litres (1–5 gal) of must.

A Burgundy yeast will, of course, not produce a Burgundy by itself unless the ingredients are suitable. Therefore a Burgundy or port yeast brings out the latent qualities of elderberries or damsons, a Sauternes yeast will do the same for peaches and gooseberries while a Hock yeast is a good choice for a delicate, light wine made from apricots or flowers.

The beginner may well start off with the single purchase of a jar of general-purpose wine yeast and employ the more specialized types when his demands, and his palate, have become more critical. Recently, different yeast strains have been combined in several new products including 'Super Yeast'. It has a fast and vigorous rate of fermentation, tolerates a higher proportion of alcohol and leaves firmer (and thus more easily discarded) lees than any other single strain of yeast. Many laboratories are engaged in yeast research and it is very likely that yeasts may become available in the near future which tolerate 20% alcohol or more.

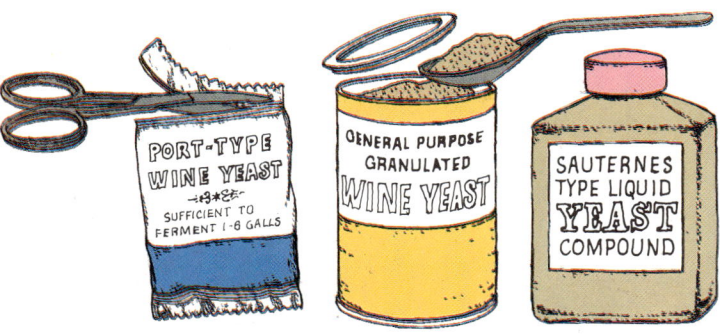

PORT-TYPE WINE YEAST
SUFFICIENT TO FERMENT 1-6 GALLS

GENERAL PURPOSE GRANULATED WINE YEAST

SAUTERNES TYPE LIQUID YEAST COMPOUND

Preparing the yeast starter

Find a small bottle with a capacity of about 0.5 litre (1 pt) – no stopper or cork will be needed. Rinse it in fairly hot water and then in the sulphite solution. Drain well.

Bring 0.25 litres ($\frac{1}{2}$ pt) of water to the boil and when cool, pour it into the now sterile bottle. Add and dissolve 1 tsp of sugar, a squirt of lemon juice, a pinch of yeast nutrient and finally the yeast. Important: make sure that the temperature of the liquid is no higher than 27°C (80°F) or the yeast cells may die. Finally, plug the mouth of the bottle with cotton wool.

After about six hours, the liquid surface should show a white ring of fine bubbles. If it does not, agitate the bottle vigorously a few times.

The yeast cells in the packet you bought will only number a few thousand at first so starting the yeast off in a kind of nursery allows the cells to become active and increase to a few million. When the starter is then added to the must, the yeast will attack the sugar at once, so reducing the period when the must is inert and at risk from bacteria. Yeast survives at a wide range of temperatures but there are limits: below about 10°C (50°F) it becomes inactive but beware of temperatures above 27°C (80°F) when the yeast cells actually die.

During the first few days the yeast cells multiply energetically, feeding on the sugar and the oxygen in the must. The yeast population increases to some 3,000,000 cells per 30 ml (1 fl oz). This first tumultuous stage of fermentation is the 'initial' fermentation and its purpose is simply to create a thriving yeast colony in preparation for the next stage.

Once you have an actively fermenting must, a portion of it can serve to inoculate other fresh musts so that the one original starter ferments one must after another. Alternatively, make up the yeast starter with twice the amount of water or fruit juice and after you have used half the liquid for the first must, top up the starter with water plus 1 tsp of sugar and a pinch of nutrient in readiness for the next must.

small photographic thermometers are very handy

water

sugar

nutrient

yeast

cotton wool

store at no more than 27°C

ready for use the next day

Nutrients for a successful fermentation

Apart from sugar, yeast cells need traces of certain minerals to thrive, traces which are present in grape juice but are often lacking in fruit musts. An absence of these minerals, commonly called nutrients, slows yeast activity and the yeast colony may fail to reach its maximum alcohol tolerance. To overcome this, most winemakers add a supply of yeast nutrients to every must, even to one that already contains them since a slight excess does not affect the quality of the wine.

The nutrients most often lacking in fruit are nitrogen, phosphate and vitamin B_1, and a combination of all three can be bought ready-made as 'yeast-nutrients' of which normally one teaspoon should be added to 4.5 litres (1 gal) of must before adding the yeast. If you are making a large amount of wine, it is cheaper to buy the materials separately at a chemist, and a jar of each should last for many seasons.

250g jar Ammonium Phosphate $(NH_4)_2HPO_4$	use $\frac{1}{2}$ tsp minimum per 4.5 litres (1 gallon) of must.
125g jar Potassium Phosphate K_2HPO_4	use $\frac{1}{4}$ tsp minimum per 4.5 litres (1 gallon) of must.
about 500 vitamin B_1 tablets each of 3 mgs	add 2 tablets to 4.5 litres (1 gal) of flower wine and 1 tablet to the same amount of fruit wine.

When the must is being moved from the mash-tun to the fermenter, adding an extra vitamin B_1 tablet will give the yeast a boost so that it ferments vigorously.

Fermentation – how it works

What is called 'fermentation' is in reality only part of the much larger process by which nature breaks down all redundant vegetable substances. The yeast fungus converts (or breaks down) the natural sugars of vegetable matter into alcohol and carbon dioxide and if this process were not isolated by excluding air by means of the airlock and later through bottling, other yeasts and bacteria would soon take over and continue the action, eventually reducing the wine to water and gas. The complete process is a complex chain of events, and has only recently been fully understood.

$$C_6H_{12}O_6 \xrightarrow{\text{fermentation}} 2C_2H_5OH + 2CO_2$$

sugar   fermentation   ethyl alcohol   carbon dioxide

Once the yeast has been added, the must will ferment vigorously during the following days, the 'initial' or tumultuous period. Do not forget to stir the must at least three times a day to prevent the formation of a cap of pulp on the surface, which would dry out and harbour bacteria. Keep the mash-tun at a temperature of 22°C (70°F).

After the pulp has been strained out, the 'slow' or sustained fermentation is carried out in the fermenter with the airlock fitted and the vessel kept at about 16°C (60°F).

Now that the yeast has had its oxygen supply cut off, it turns to the sugar for food and converts it into carbon dioxide – the bubbles passing out through the airlock – and alcohol. During this second fermentation period the yeast colony does not multiply any further, which is why it was so important to create a thriving colony in the first stage.

Check that the level of the liquid in the fermenter is not higher than the shoulder of the vessel, otherwise some froth may be driven up into the airlock and block it. The fermentation may end after three weeks in the case of light dry wines, but it may take another month or longer for full-bodied wines. Do not worry if it seems to be taking a long time – a slow and steady fermentation will usually produce a superior wine.

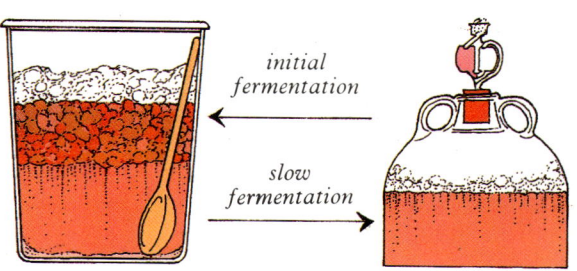

initial fermentation

slow fermentation

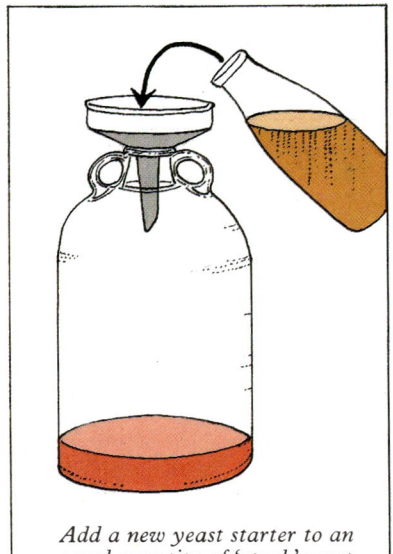

Add a new yeast starter to an equal quantity of 'stuck' must

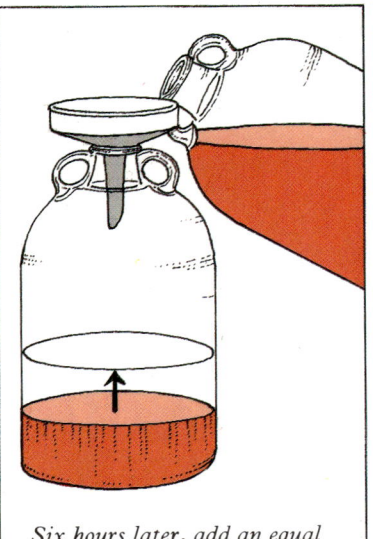

Six hours later, add an equal amount of must again . . .

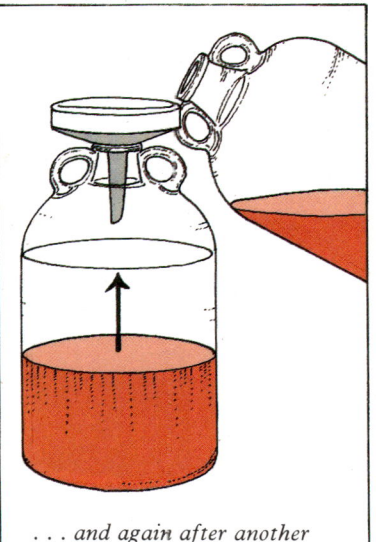

. . . and again after another six hours . . .

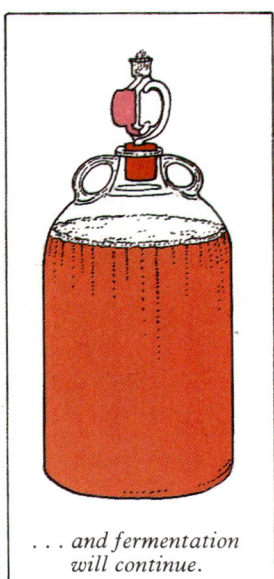

. . . and fermentation will continue.

How to deal with a stuck fermentation

Yeast needs a controlled environment in which to thrive and multiply: it needs sugar (but not too much), warmth (not more than 22°C (70°F), oxygen at the beginning, plenty of nutrients and the correct amounts of acids and tannin. A recipe should include all these elements in the right proportion or the fermentation may 'stick', something that even experienced wine-makers have to deal with from time to time.

Too large a proportion of sugar is often the result of starting a must with too little water so that the sugar concentration is too high, so check your data on ingredients or use the hydrometer.

Other causes may be: too little sugar (check the data sheet and add more if needed), wrong temperature, lack of acids or nutrients (check and add), lack of oxygen (aerate by decanting and prolonged stirring) and too much alcohol, in which case the wine *is* finished. If a ferment sticks towards the end of the fermentation, it is better to accept it as the sweet wine it is and to use it for blending later on.

Sometimes a ferment will not even get under way, in which case the yeast must be checked – it may be too old and no longer potent. Make up another yeast starter from the same batch of yeast and wait for it to show the typical ring of bubbles. If it does, the yeast is all right, but do not add it to the must straight away: use it as explained below.

After you have checked any other possible short-comings (sugar, temperature, nutrients etc) and the fermentation remains inactive for the next day or two, it must be re-started with a fresh yeast colony. First ensure that the sugar content does not exceed 1 kilo per 4.5 litres (2 lb per 1 gal) and dilute if necessary. Use the yeast starter prepared earlier or make up a fresh one and when it actively ferments, add to it an equal quantity of must, shake it thoroughly now and then and allow it to stand at 22°C (70°F) until this too ferments (the first signs should appear after 6 hours). Repeat the procedure by again mixing an equal amount of must with the starter until all of the stuck wine is fermenting once more.

43

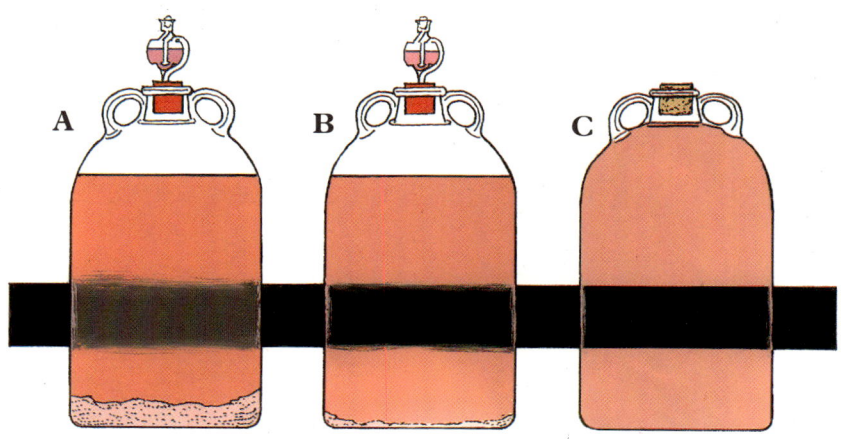

A) *Wine just before the first racking. (For sweet wines add one sulphite tablet).*

B) *Just before the second racking. (Another sulphite tablet should be added for sweet wines). The wine should also be topped up.*

C) *The wine becomes bright and transparent after further rackings.*

When to rack

Apart from fermentation, racking is the most important factor affecting the quality of a wine. It is vital not to delay the first racking unduly since off-flavours from decomposing plant matter and decaying yeast cells can develop quickly.

When the ferment has slowed down and shows a bubble only every 60 seconds or so, rack the wine if the taste is acceptable, but if you want a dry wine, wait until the airlock action has stopped completely. See page 29 for sugar feeding. If you are using a hydrometer, check the specific gravity and terminate the fermentation at these gravities:

dry white and red wines	995–1000
medium and sweet table wines	1005–1010
dessert wines	1010–1020

After the first racking, the fermenter will need to be topped up and, if it is to be a sweet wine, the topping-up water may contain up to 110 g (4 oz) of sugar, plus 1 or 2 sulphite tablets to terminate fermentation. If it is to be a dry wine, top up with wine from last year or with sterile water, although this will dilute the wine a little. The racked wine will still be milky or cloudy because it contains some yeast and plant-matter held in suspension.

Light and dry wines will clear about two weeks after the first racking, when the remaining particles settle at the bottom of the fermenter as lees. Medium and sweet wines may need more time to clear and plums in particular require perhaps an extra month or two. The dead yeast cells which form this second sediment are 'autolysing' – they are decomposing and passing their substances (some beneficial and some not) into the wine. To prevent this from going too far, a second racking is now necessary but with a little difference.

Whereas during the first racking the wine could be allowed to splash into the new vessel and thus absorb fresh oxygen, the second racking should proceed quietly. This means that the pouring end of the syphon should be submerged so that splashing (and over-oxidising) is avoided. The wine can now be topped up with wine from last year or sterile water but not with sugar-water since this would prolong the ferment indefinitely. Some winemakers prefer to drop sterilised glass marbles into the fermenter, so raising the level of the liquid. After racking, the fermenter (still sealed with its airlock) can be placed in a much lower temperature of between 5–10°C (40–50°F) to help clarification.

All wines will profit from at least two more rackings at 2 to 3 monthly intervals (two months in summer, three in winter); racking helps to stabilize the wine and reduces the risk of a fermentation re-starting after bottling which would lead to bottles bursting under pressure. From the third racking onwards, $\frac{1}{2}$ or 1 crushed sulphite tablet per 4.5 litres (1 gal) should be placed in the fresh storage vessel so that the emitted gas prevents spoilage bacteria from entering during the operation.

Wine disorders and their cure

Pectin haze. If a pectin haze develops despite the earlier addition of a pectin-destroying enzyme (see page 38), first test for pectin. Pour 90 ml (3 fl oz) of methylated spirit into a measure and add 30 ml (1 fl oz) of the suspect wine. Shake the jar and if jelly-like clots or strings are formed, the haze is caused by pectin. If there is no immediate reaction, let the jar stand for an hour or two in case there is only a slight presence of pectin. Treatment: add 1 tsp Pectozyme or Pectinol to 4.5 litres (1 gal) of wine and if the haze persists, repeat the dose after the next racking.

Starch hazes. Test for the presence of starch by adding a few drops of iodine to 15 ml ($\frac{1}{2}$ fl oz) of the suspect wine and if starch is present, the sample will develop a deep blue-black colour. Treatment: add 1 tsp Amylozyme 100 or Fungal Amylase 2209 to 4.5 litres (1 gal) of wine and place the fermenter for a week in a temperature of 24°C (75°F).

Coloured hazes may be caused by a metallic contamination and are often white, purple or brown. Iron and copper hazes can sometimes be cleared for a time by adding $\frac{1}{2}$ tsp of citric acid powder to every 4.5 litre (1 gal) of must.

Darkening of the wine can result from contact with iron (see 'coloured hazes') or more commonly through oxidation from mouldy fruit. Add 2 sulphite tablets to stabilise the wine and do not drink it for at least two months so that the sulphite effect has time to wear off.

Other hazes, taints and smells, not easily identified, may result from bacteria, damaged fruit, proximity of plastic containers to petrol, onions etc. Treatment: use sulphite first and if unsuccessful, fine with Bentonite (see page 46).

Acetification is the turning of wine into vinegar. It is caused through contamination by the fruit-fly or by airborne spores of vinegar yeast that have entered the wine – usually during must-straining or racking operations. It is easily detected by a vinegary smell and acid taste, both of which increase until the wine has entirely become vinegar. There is no treatment for this, so either use it in the kitchen as wine-vinegar or pour it away, but remember it is vital to clean and sterilize every vessel and piece of equipment that was in contact with the infected wine to prevent the bacteria from surviving and spreading.

Flowers of wine appear as white flecks or a white film on the surface of the wine. They are caused by the *Mycoderma* bacteria and sometimes form when a vessel is not topped up sufficiently. If the film is thick, the wine is beyond remedy and must be poured away, but if it is noticed in the early stages, remove as much of the growth as possible, then filter the wine through a fine cloth and add 1 crushed sulphite tablet to 4.5 litres (1 gal). A simple way to remove surface film and dirt is to float it out. Syphon into the vessel a little extra wine or water. As the liquid surface reaches the top of the vessel, any film or dirt will float up and will be carried out. The wine will not keep for very long, however.

Mousiness is a strong mouldy or mouse-like smell and a drop of the wine rubbed into the palm of your hand radiates the odour like perfume. Treatment: 1 sulphite tablet per 4.5 litres (1 gal) in the early stages will arrest the disorder, and aeration before drinking reduces the smell, but an advanced infection cannot be cured.

Mustiness is often caused by dirty fermenters or by letting the wine stand too long on the lees. Treatment: rack at once, aerate the wine and add 1 sulphite tablet.

Medicinal flavour usually results from lack of acids in the wine. Add 1 tsp of mixed acids (see page 33) and store the wine at least 6 months before drinking.

Ropiness or oiliness appears as rope-like threads in the wine, irridescent waves, or as a layer of oil on its surface, and is caused by the tartarophtorum bacteria. Treatment: pour the wine into the mash-tun and stir it thoroughly. Filter it back into the fermenter through a fine cloth and add 2 sulphite tablets per 4.5 litres (1 gal).

Over-sweetness and low alcohol content are the result of a stuck ferment. Treatment: restart fermentation (see page 43).

Sulphite taste and smell disappears with keeping and should any be present, it simply means that the wine is not ready for drinking.

45

Finishing the wine

Fining and filtering

It is always better to let wines clear by themselves without either fining or filtering since both these processes, whilst removing obstinate hazes, also take out other valuable ingredients.

When a wine shows no improvement after 5–6 rackings and after being kept cool for a few months, begin by fining, since it is less harmful than filtering. Fining removes very tiny particles that may pass through all but the most stringent filters.

Always use a minimum of fining agent as otherwise the haze may be stabilized instead of being removed. Professional winemakers use mineral finings such as Bentonite, kaolin or kieselguhr as well as organic finings like gelatine, isinglass, egg-white or casein.

Bentonite, a powdered montmorillonite clay, is one of the safest and most effective fining agents the amateur can use – safest because an overdose of it does not harm the wine. Mix 5 g ($\frac{1}{8}$ oz) Bentonite in 100 ml ($3\frac{1}{2}$ fl oz) boiled, then cooled, water. Strain the slurry through a

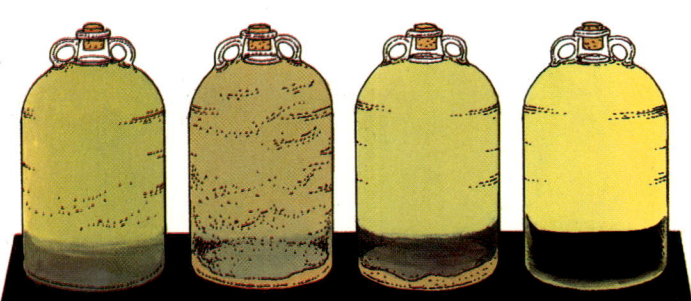

fine sieve to remove any lumps and pour it into a sterile screw-cap bottle. Let it stand for 24 hours. Rack the wine and pour one third of the slurry into it. Shake the fermenter a number of times at 5-minute intervals so that the slurry mixes well with the wine. Let it stand and rack it after a month and if the wine is still hazy, repeat the treatment with the remainder of the slurry.

Filtering should only be tried as a last resort to clear a hazy wine. Simple filtering by straining through a few layers of a fine cloth takes a long time, during which the wine is at risk from bacteria. The best filters on the market are costly and justified only when more than 20 litres (5 gal) at a time need to be cleared.

Closed filters can operate unattended overnight – they are equipped with silicon-fibre pads (instead of the older asbestos fibre) and while the path of the liquid inside the filter is excluded from air, over-oxidation may occur as the wine drops from the filter bed into the fermenter. This disadvantage can be overcome to some extent by passing the wine through a tube all the way – see opposite page.

Vacuum filters are the best but also the most expensive filters on the market. In these, the domestic water supply operates a water pump which creates a vacuum that sucks wine through the filter pad at a faster rate. Since the rate is faster, however, clarification is not 100% and very cloudy wines may have to be passed through more than once.

Whichever filter has been used, the wine has to be topped up afterwards to the maximum level possible, heavily sulphited and left to recuperate at a low temperature until the next racking.

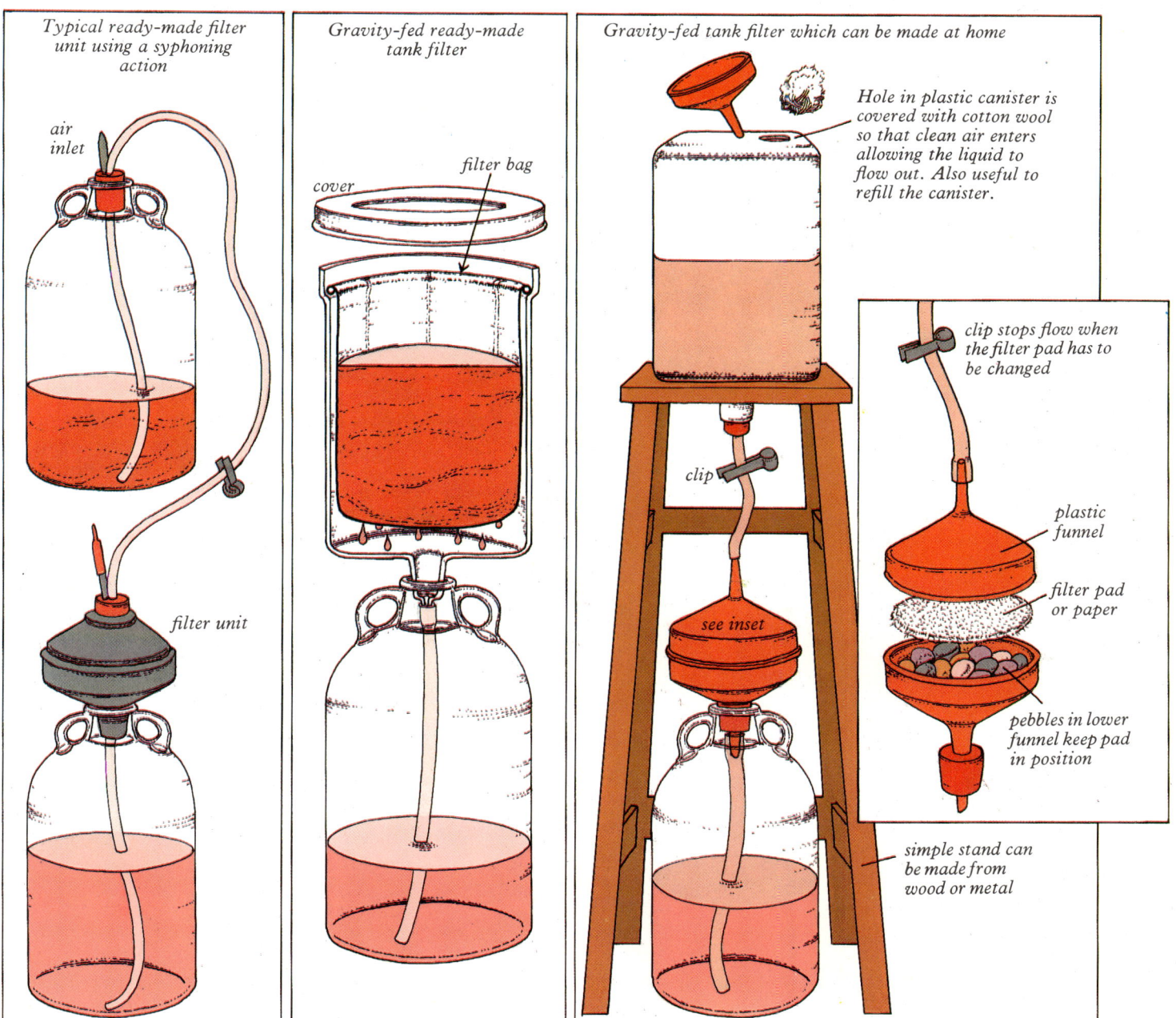

Typical ready-made filter unit using a syphoning action

air inlet

filter unit

Gravity-fed ready-made tank filter

cover

filter bag

Gravity-fed tank filter which can be made at home

Hole in plastic canister is covered with cotton wool so that clean air enters allowing the liquid to flow out. Also useful to refill the canister.

clip

see inset

simple stand can be made from wood or metal

clip stops flow when the filter pad has to be changed

plastic funnel

filter pad or paper

pebbles in lower funnel keep pad in position

47

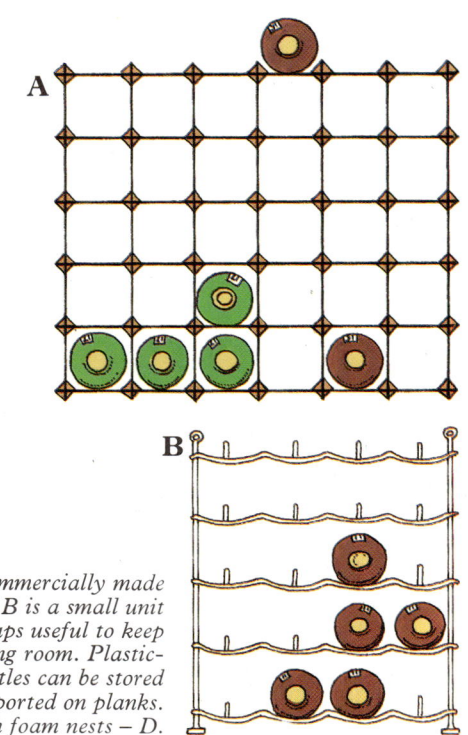

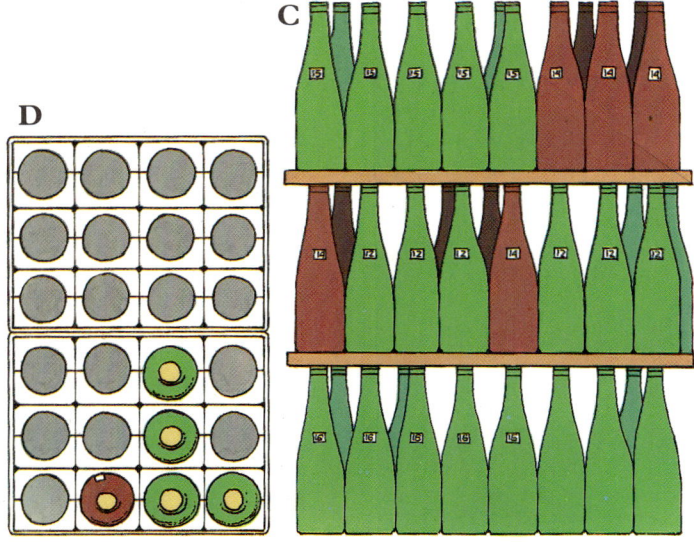

A and B are commercially made wine racks – B is a small unit which is perhaps useful to keep bottles in a dining room. Plastic-stoppered bottles can be stored upright (C), supported on planks. Wine cartons with foam nests – D.

Bottling, storing and cellaring

The practical winemaker bottles most of his wine only just before the new vintage requires the fermenting and storing space. The exception is the maturing of red wines and special whites, for which extra casks or storage vessels should be made available since all wines mature better in bulk.

Wash, sulphite and drain corks and bottles – a wooden draining board with pegs as shown will be invaluable if you plan to bottle a large amount of wine. Fill the bottles by syphoning the wine and let the liquid level rise to about 20 mm ($\frac{3}{4}$ in) from the rim. Wine bottles that have been sealed with cylindrical corks or cork-stoppers should be stored on their side so that the cork remains in contact with the wine, stays moist and swollen and does not dry out. For these bottles, a storage bin or bottle rack is not a luxury but a necessity.

Many types of storage rack are now available quite cheaply, ready-made units as well as all kinds of systems designed for self-assembly. Empty wine cartons also make useful racks and a few coats of paint will give them a longer life. Very often they are fitted inside with plastic foam nests in which the bottles of home-made wine rest, and this expanded polystyrene foam will insulate the wine to an extent against rapid changes in temperature. Bottles that have been sealed with plastic stoppers can safely be stored upright and, instead of in a bottle rack, can be stacked in tiers by the use of a few loose planks.

Whatever the shelving method employed, wine should be stored at about 5–10°C (40–50°F) in a dark place free from vibration. If a window is near, cover the storage rack with a dark cloth to prevent light from falling onto the winebottles continuously. It is also a good idea to keep a small storage rack in your dining area where red wines can acquire room temperature. That way, if you are gripped by a sudden desire for wine with your meal, there is no need for a journey down draughty steps into a cold cellar, or for drastic attempts to warm the wine suddenly.

Tasting, blending and serving wine

Sweet, sour, salt and bitter are the major tastes we detect physiologically although our mouth experiences

A pipette makes it easy to draw small samples of wine from a storage vessel or cask.

many other sensations such as temperature and texture. Food as well as wine gives us experiences of these sensations which we find satisfying. Taste buds do not convey the same experience to everybody and what tastes pleasant and just right to one person may need to be adjusted if it is to please another. Even one individual's palate is not satisfied with the same drink throughout the day – his metabolism has different needs from morning to evening. For instance, if you rack and taste wine early in the morning it will appear more acid than when you do so after a meal or later in the day.

The pleasure of drinking wine is also influenced by the weather. Wine not only seems to 'breathe' more out in the open on a sunny day, but the drinker himself absorbs it with more gusto and satisfaction than if he were to drink it on a rainy and depressing evening indoors. Few people feel brave enough in those circumstances to contemplate a young and sharp wine, even if it is served with a delicious lobster Thermidor à la

bonne femme. That is why it makes sense to stock more of the lighter wines for summer drinking and reserve the full-bodied or sweeter wines for the colder winter days when our bodies need more calories.

Home-made wines can be designed to cater for many of these requirements and an excellent method of adding variety is the *blending* of finished wines. Another advantage is that a perfect wine may often be the result of blending two or more wines that are imperfect in some way and that is why it has been suggested at various stages in the book that the odd quantity of over-sweet or over-acid wine should simply be put by. Small measures of these wines may provide just the element that is lacking in an otherwise perfect wine from another batch. While the beginner may perhaps have produced such wines by accident, the advanced winemaker will deliberately set out to make blending wines and store them for future use.

Common faults in home-made wines are over-acidity (mask it with a bland wine), over-sweetness (add some acid wine or one rich in tannin) and lack of nose or bouquet (add flower wine). Good-tasting but bad-smelling wines become acceptable in the following way: aerate the wine by decanting and cool it in the refrigerator for a few hours before drinking, then when you pour it into glasses ready for the meal, add to each glass a slightly younger but warmer flower wine. Since the faulty wine is cold, its smell will be subdued but the flowers in the warm wine breathe and send out their aroma.

Do not, however, try to cure a tainted wine by blending since it is most likely that the sound wine will become tainted as well – it is better in a case like this to write the spoilt wine off.

Blending sessions can be very enjoyable affairs. Your family or friends will be delighted to help assess the wines you have produced and to suggest and try out blends to overcome possible shortcomings. The wines need not be tested in bulk since small measures are sufficient to establish the best proportions for blending. You will need a number of clean wine glasses, some of which are filled with the sample wines; a calibrated measure; a notepad; some plain bread with which to neutralise the palate and a glass or two of the best of your last year's wine or a commercial grape wine of the type you normally prefer.

Take a mouthful of the best or commercial wine – it will set a standard for the tests to come. Hold it in your mouth and 'chew' or swirl it. It may make you cough at first but try to suck in a little air through your teeth to aerate the wine in your mouth and bring out the aroma. Then drink it. A well-balanced wine will taste sharp on the top of your tongue and sweet on the back of the throat. Tannin will feel bitter on the sides of your mouth, while the gums detect alcohol as a stinging or prickling sensation. Nibble some bread.

Now test one of your own wines that needs improving. Hold the filled glass in front of a window or a light. Does the wine look clear and bright? How does it smell? How does it taste? Write the assessments down on the notepad. Since it is bound to be a young wine and may be harsh, acid or too sweet, you had better spit it out. Make the same test with the wine intended for blending and follow it with a nibble of bread and a sip of the 'best' wine.

Half-fill the measure with the faulty wine and add to it a small quantity, perhaps $\frac{1}{8}$ part of the blending wine. Taste it to check how the wine has changed. Take time over this. Add more if you think it needs more and when the right proportion has been found, note it down and enter the results on a new data sheet.

Finally (and often many hours later), blend the bulk of the faulty wine with the established portion of the blending wine in the mash-tun and return the new blend to the fermenters, fit airlocks and attach new labels. Blended wines should be treated as new wines since they sometimes begin to ferment again. Do not worry about this but welcome it since it means that the two wines are marrying properly to form a new wine. Rack after two months and at least twice more at three-monthly intervals. Use this list of terms to describe a wine for your wine diary:

Appearance

Colour:	purplish – ruby – red – brick-red – brownish rosé – salmon – pale pink – greeny-white – pale yellow – golden yellow – deep gold – brownish.
Richness:	depth of colour – fullness of flow
Brilliance:	clear – hazy – cloudy – with floating deposits

Nose

Floweriness:	spring flowers – summer flowers – autumn leaves
Fruitiness:	soft fruits – stone-fruits – apples and pears
Spiciness:	cinnamon – vanilla – peppery
Herbiness:	thyme – lavender – bay – rosemary
Earthiness:	slaty – smoky – flinty – peaty
Yeastiness:	strong – subdued

Taste

Taste buds:	sweet – acid – bitter – salt
Other sensations:	rough – smooth/round – sharp/thin – full/warmth – coolness
Remarks	too young – young and fresh – ready to drink – better in X years – mature – will keep for Y years – over the top – worn out.

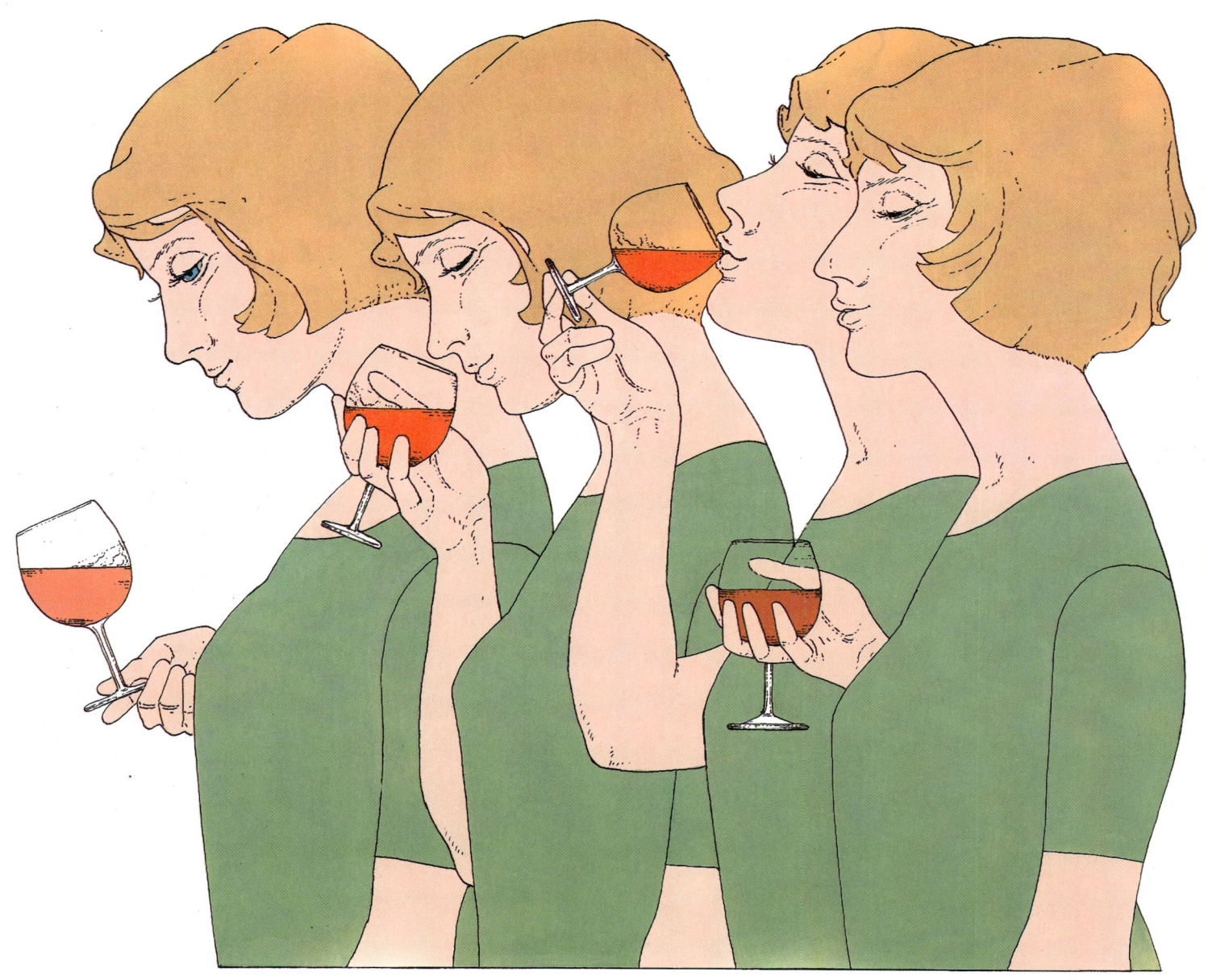

Look! Hold the glass
against something
white.

Sniff! The warmth of
your hand will strengthen
the bouquet.

Sip once or twice to convey
the wine to different regions
of the mouth

Finally taste! Aerate the
wine in the mouth and
drink it.

Serving your table wine is the moment for which all the foregoing has been a preparation – it is the moment of truth! It is well worth selecting a day for this when the wine has the chance to accompany a meal that will match its quality. So take a bottle from its storage and stand it upright for a day so that any sediment will fall to the bottom of the bottle. If your red wine is stored in a very cold place, bring it to the dining room at least a week before serving so that it gently warms to room temperature. If you want to serve red wine at short notice, do not place the bottle in hot water (which would harm the bouquet): serve it from a warmed decanter and ask your guests to warm it in the glass with their hands, serving small measures first which warm more quickly.

White wines should be served chilled but not frozen and an hour in the refrigerator (not the freezer, in which bottles may burst) is quite sufficient. A wine-cooler or ice bucket is not only a decorative but also an efficient container for cooling wine on a warm summer day. If it is deep enough for the liquid to cover most of the length of the bottle, it need not be packed with very much ice. Fill it with cold water almost to the rim and let about ten pieces of ice float in it: then the wine should be ready for drinking within thirty minutes or so.

Alas, pretentious wine glasses or inherited silver goblets prevent many people from enjoying wine properly. Avoid coloured, over-decorated or 'precious' crystal glasses since their thick or knobbly rims may disturb the intimate contact between your lips and the wine. The cheapest wine glasses are often the best and ordinary goblets of the type used in restaurants allow you to taste wine to its best advantage.

Wine glasses should be clear, so that the colour of the wine can be appreciated; they should be tulip-shaped, so that they conserve the aroma; they should be made of thin glass, so that the hand can warm a red wine and those for white wines should have a long stem, so that the hand does not warm the wine or become chilled by its coolness. Fill the glasses to about half their capacity so that the upper, empty half cradles the aroma.

Home-made wines are usually stronger in alcohol than wines that have been bought in a shop and it is a matter of courtesy to offer water with the wine particularly to guests who may have to drive. If the water is served in a carafe, they can then dilute the wine according to their own needs.

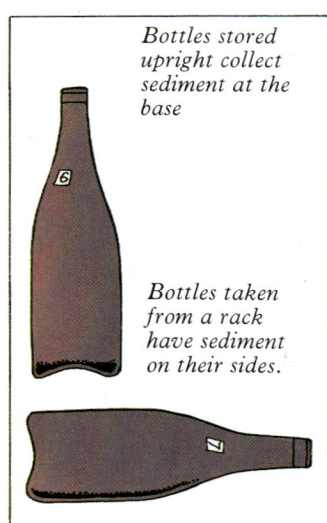
Bottles stored upright collect sediment at the base

Bottles taken from a rack have sediment on their sides.

For decanting, open the bottle and let it rest for a few hours in a basket so that the sediment forms as shown.

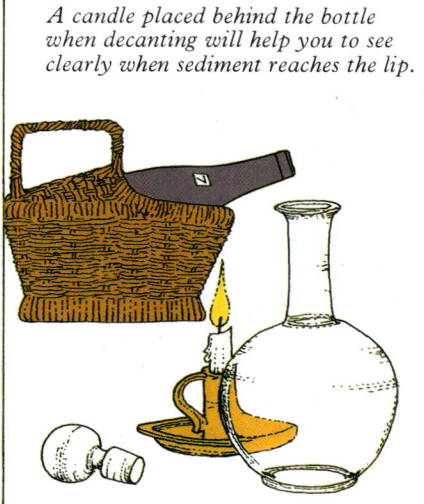
A candle placed behind the bottle when decanting will help you to see clearly when sediment reaches the lip.

Red wines can be insulated against the cooling effect of marble or glass table tops with coasters and mats.

Paris goblet for red and some white wines

Baccarat glass for the finest reds and whites

German wine glass for cool whites and rosé.

Sherry glass – the 'Copita'

Port glass, also useful for tasting cognac

The Champagne flute

It is better to wash glasses in hot water only; soap or detergent may leave a bad-tasting film.

53

Recipes

The recipes on the following pages are for wines that are well balanced and not difficult to make. You might start with the easier ones with fruit juices from the supermarket, but as your wine-making progresses and your taste sharpens, you may want to try combinations of ingredients different from those set out in the recipes.

Whenever you try a new combination, ask yourself the following questions to establish whether the wine will be well balanced or 'round': will the wine have body, flavour and bouquet and what is the most complementary amount of alcohol, acid and tannin?

A balanced wine has 'roundness' or vinosity which is achieved often by the inclusion of a small measure of grape concentrate, raisins or sultanas and if you are short of one or the other, or do not want the extra expense, replace 0.5 litres (1 pt) of the concentrate with 1 kilo (2 lb) of raisins. When you invent your own recipes, do make allowance for the natural sugar content of both ingredients: 0.5 litres (1 pt) of grape concentrate is usually equivalent to 450 g (1 lb) of sugar while 450 g (1 lb) of raisins will contain between 270–300 g (9–11 oz) of natural sugar.

The quantities are given in both metric and British Imperial and the metric volumes have been rounded up for convenience. If you make wine in America, the liquid measures in the recipes need to be converted as the U.S. gallon is smaller than the British: 1 British gallon equals 1.2 (1 1/5th) U.S. gallons.

All recipes are designed to produce 4½ litres or 1 gallon of wine.

The ingredients in this section are readily available at supermarkets, greengrocers or winemaker's shops, enabling you to make wine throughout the year.

Since most of the ingredients have already been processed into fruit juice, canned fruits or grape concentrates, little work is required to prepare musts from them. Fruit juices can be bought canned, frozen or as a syrup. Remember that you can always replace grape concentrate with raisins or sultanas (see page 55).

Easy grape wine *(medium white table wine)*

1000 g	white grape concentrate	$1\frac{3}{4}$	pints
450 g	granulated sugar	1	lb
450 g	peeled bananas	1	lb
2.5 ml	malic acid	$\frac{1}{2}$	tsp
2.5 ml	citric acid	$\frac{1}{2}$	tsp
5 ml	pectic enzyme	1	tsp
	general purpose or Chablis yeast and nutrients		
	sulphite tablets		

1) Make up the yeast starter (see page 41).
2) Next day slice the bananas and boil in 2 litres ($3\frac{1}{2}$ pts) of water for 20 minutes. Place the sugar in the mash-tun. Strain (do not press) the hot banana liquid over the sugar and stir until it has dissolved. Add the grape concentrate, the acids and nutrients and make up the must to about 4 litres (7 pts) with sterile (previously boiled) water. When the must has cooled to 22°C (70°F), add the enzyme and the yeast and stir. Cover the mash-tun and ferment for 5 days, stirring once a day.
3) Strain the must into the sterilised fermenter and fit airlock. Ferment to dryness or, if you want a sweeter wine, rack when a bubble appears only every minute (SG 1000-1005).
4) Rack for the second time when the wine is really clear and top up. Store at 10°C (50°F) for 9 months, racking and sulphiting ($\frac{1}{2}$ tablet) every 3 months. Bottle when no sediment appears and store for 6 months.

Easy apricot wine *(dry white table wine)*

450 g	dried apricots	1	lb
500 ml	white grape concentrate	1	pint
14 g	dried elderflowers or rose petals	$\frac{1}{2}$	oz
570 g	honey	$1\frac{1}{4}$	lb
5 ml	grape tannin	1	tsp
5 ml	pectic enzyme	1	tsp
	Bordeaux yeast and nutrients		
	sulphite tablets		

1) Prepare the yeast starter (see page 41). Wash and chop the apricots and place them with the grape concentrate, honey and flowers in the mash-tun. Cover with $3\frac{1}{2}$ litres ($6\frac{1}{2}$ pts) of warm water. Stir until the honey has dissolved, add 2 sulphite tablets and cover.
2) Next day add the other ingredients and ferment the must at 22°C (70°F) for 4 days. Stir twice daily.
3) Strain must into the fermenter, fit airlock and ferment to dryness (SG 995) then rack.
4) Rack for the second time when the wine is really clear. Store at 10°C (50°F) for a year, racking and sulphiting ($\frac{1}{2}$ tablet) every 3 months. Bottle and keep for 6 months.

Apricot wine *(light dry table wine)*

1000 g	canned apricots in syrup (adjust if unsweetened)	2	lb
225 g	white grape concentrate	$\frac{1}{2}$	lb
450 g	granulated sugar	1	lb
2.5 ml	tartaric acid	$\frac{1}{2}$	tsp
2.5 ml	citric acid	$\frac{1}{2}$	tsp
5 ml	grape tannin	1	tsp
5 ml	pectic enzyme	1	tsp
	Hock or Chablis yeast and nutrients		
	sulphite tablets		

1) Make up the yeast starter (see page 41). Pour apricots and syrup into the mash-tun. Add the other ingredients, except the yeast, plus 2 sulphite tablets. Cover and leave overnight.
2) Next day stir in the yeast and ferment for 4 days at 22°C (70°F) stirring daily.
3) Press the pulp in a nylon bag and strain into the fermenter. Fit airlock and ferment to dryness (SG 995).
4) Rack, and repeat as soon as the wine is really clear. Store at 10°C (50°F) for 6 months, racking and sulphiting ($\frac{1}{2}$ tablet) every third month. If no sediment appears, bottle and keep for another 3 months.

Crushing sulphite tablets between teaspoons

Apricot wine (*sweet white after-dinner wine*)

450 g	dried apricots	1 lb
450 g	sultanas or raisins	1 lb
340 g	overripe peeled bananas	¾ lb
14 g	dried elderflowers	½ oz
900 g	granulated sugar	2 lb
5 ml	grape tannin	1 tsp
2.5 ml	tartaric acid	½ tsp
2.5 ml	citric acid	½ tsp
5 ml	pectic enzyme	1 tsp
	super or Madeira yeast and nutrients	
	sulphite tablets	

1) Prepare yeast starter (see page 41). Wash and chop the apricots, mince the sultanas and place both with half the sugar in the mash-tun. Boil the bananas in 2 litres (3½ pts) of water for 20 minutes then strain the hot liquid into the mash-tun. Stir until the sugar has dissolved and make up the must to 4 litres (7 pts). Cool and add 1 sulphite tablet.
2) Next day add the other ingredients except the rest of the sugar and ferment at 22°C (70°F) for 4 days.
3) Press the pulp lightly and strain the liquid into the fermenter. Fit airlock. When fermentation slows, sugar-feed the rest of the sugar in 113 g (4 oz) quantities, adding the last portion shortly before racking (SG 1020).
4) Rack and add 2 sulphite tablets. Rack again when the wine is really clear. Store at 10°C (50°F) for one year, racking and sulphiting (½ tablet) every 3 months. Bottle and store for a year at least.

Gooseberry wine (*dry white table wine*)

450 g	can unsweetened gooseberries	1 lb
900 g	granulated sugar	2 lb
500 ml	white grape concentrate	1 pint
5 ml	pectic enzyme	1 tsp
	juice of 1 lemon	
	general purpose yeast starter, nutrients	
	sulphite tablets	

1) Prepare the yeast starter (see page 41). Mash the gooseberries by hand and place them with the syrup in the mash-tun. Add all the sugar and pour 2 litres (3½ pts) boiling water onto the must. Cover and let it cool.
2) Next day add the other ingredients and make up the must to 4 litres (7 pts). Ferment for 4 days at 22°C (70°F), stirring twice daily.
3) Lightly press the gooseberries in a strainer and pour the clear must into the fermenter. Fit airlock and ferment almost to dry (SG about 1000).
4) Rack into clean vessel and when the wine is really clear, rack again. Store at 10°C (50°F) for 6 months. Rack twice more, adding ½ sulphite tablet each time. Bottle and store for 6 months.

Sultana wine (*medium white table wine*)

1360 g	washed sultanas or raisins	3 lb
340 g	honey	¾ lb
14 g	dried elderflowers	½ oz
5 ml	grape tannin	1 tsp
2.5 ml	citric acid	½ tsp
2.5 ml	tartaric acid	½ tsp
5 ml	pectic enzyme	1 tsp
	Hock or Bordeaux yeast and nutrients	
	sulphite tablets	

1) Prepare the yeast starter (see page 41). Mince or chop the sultanas and place them with the honey in the mash-tun. Pour 4 litres (7 pts) warm water over the must and stir until the honey has dissolved. Add 2 sulphite tablets, stir and cover.
2) The next day add the other ingredients and ferment on the pulp for 4 days at 22°C (70°F), stirring 3 times daily.
3) Press the pulp lightly and strain the liquid into the fermenter, fit airlock and ferment almost to dryness (SG 1005).
4) Rack and add 1 sulphite tablet. Rack again as soon as the wine is really clear. Store at 10°C (50°F) for another 6 months, racking and sulphiting (½ tablet) twice more at least. Bottle and store for 6 months.

Sultana wine *(sweet white after-dinner wine)*

1360 g	washed sultanas or raisins	3	lb
680 g	granulated sugar	1½	lb
14 g	dried elderflowers	½	oz
5 ml	citric acid	1	tsp
2.5 ml	tartaric acid	½	tsp
5 ml	grape tannin	1	tsp
5 ml	pectic enzyme	1	tsp
	Madeira or Sauternes yeast and nutrients		
	sulphite tablets		

1) Prepare the yeast starter (see page 41). Mince or chop the sultanas and place them with 225 g (½ lb) sugar in the mash-tun. Boil 3 litres (5½ pts) of water and add, stirring until the sugar has dissolved. Make up the must to 4 litres (7 pts). Add 2 sulphite tablets, the acids, cover and let cool.
2) Next day add the other ingredients except the rest of the sugar, stir and ferment for 4 days at 22°C (70°F), stirring 3 times daily.
3) Press the pulp lightly, strain the liquid into the fermenter and fit airlock. Sugar-feed quantities of 113 g (4 oz) whenever the ferment slows, adding the last portion just before racking (SG 1015).
4) Rack and add 2 sulphite tablets. Rack again as soon as the wine is really clear and store at 10°C (50°F) for 9 months, racking and sulphiting (½ tablet) every third month. Bottle and store for at least 6 months.

Sultana wine *(strong Madeira-style social wine)*

1360 g	washed sultanas or raisins	3 lb
450 g	brown sugar, treacle or molasses	1 lb
225 g	peeled bananas	½ lb
25 g	dried elderflowers	1 oz
5 ml	tartaric acid	1 tsp
5 ml	citric acid	1 tsp
5 ml	grape tannin	1 tsp
5 ml	pectic enzyme	1 tsp
3	vitamin B_1 tablets	
	Madeira yeast and nutrients	
	sulphite tablets	

1) Make up the yeast starter (see page 41). Chop or mince the sultanas and place the puree in the mash-tun. Add the sugar. Boil the bananas for 20 minutes in 4 litres (7 pts) of water and strain the hot juice over the pulp. Stir until the sugar has dissolved. Cover and let cool overnight.
2) Next day add the other ingredients and ferment for 5 days at 22°C (70°F), stirring 3 times daily.
3) Press the must lightly and strain into the fermenter. Ensure that must is shoulder-high and top up if necessary.

Add the last vitamin tablet and fit airlock. Ferment almost to dryness.
4) Rack, and repeat as soon as the wine is really clear. Store at 10°C (50°F) for at least a year, racking and sulphiting (½ tablet) every 3 months. Bottle and store for at least another year, but any extra time will help to develop the Madeira flavour.

Pineapple wine *(medium white table wine)*

1.2 l	canned pineapple juice	2¼	pints
450 g	washed sultanas or raisins	1	lb
900 g	granulated sugar	2	lb
2.5 ml	tartaric acid	½	tsp
2.5 ml	malic acid	½	tsp
5 ml	grape tannin	1	tsp
5 ml	pectic enzyme	1	tsp
	Graves yeast and nutrients		
	sulphite tablets		

1) Prepare the yeast starter (see page 41). Mince or chop the sultanas and place the puree, the sugar and the pineapple juice in the mash-tun. Bring to the boil 2.5 litres (4 pts) of water, add the sugar and stir until dissolved. Cover and let cool overnight.
2) Next day add the other ingredients, stir and ferment at 22°C (70°F) for 3 days, stirring 3 times daily.
3) Press the residue lightly and strain the must into the fermenter. Top up to shoulder-high and fit airlock. Ferment until there is only one bubble per minute (SG 1005).
4) Rack and when the wine is really clear rack again and top up. Store at 10°C (50°F) and rack and sulphite (½ tablet) 3 times more before bottling. Bottle and keep for 3 months.

Orange wine *(light white table wine)*

0.5 l	canned or fresh orange juice	1 pint
0.5 l	white grape concentrate	1 pint
1 kg	sugar	2 lb
2.5 ml	tartaric acid	½ tsp
	pectic enzyme	
	tannin (see page 34)	
	general purpose yeast and nutrients	
	sulphite tablets	

1)   Place all the sugar in the mash-tun, add boiling water to bring the must up to 2.5 litres (5 pints). Stir until the sugar has dissolved, then add the orange juice and grape concentrate. When cooled, add the enzyme, acid, tannin, nutrients and the yeast starter (see page 41).
2)   Ferment for 3 days in the mash-tun, then strain the must into the fermenter and keep it at about 16°C (60°F) until fermentation ends (SG about 995).
3)   Rack and when the wine is clear (3–4 weeks), rack for the second time. Store at around 10°C (50°F).
4)   Rack and sulphite (1 tablet) for the third time two months later.
5)   Bottle or rack three months later and store for another 3 months.

Orange wine *(medium white apéritif wine)*

1.4 l	orange juice, unsweetened	2½ pints
0.5 l	white grape concentrate	¾ pint
340 g	peeled bananas	¾ lb
900 g	granulated sugar	2 lb
	juice and peel from 5 oranges	
5 ml	pectic enzyme	1 tsp
	Sherry yeast and nutrients	
	sulphite tablets	

1)   Prepare the yeast starter (see page 41). Slice the bananas and boil them in a saucepan for 20 minutes in 2 litres (3½ pints) of water. Pour the orange juice into the mash-tun and add the sugar. Peel the 5 oranges thinly (avoid any pith) and drop peel into mash-tun. Squeeze the oranges and add juice. Strain the hot banana liquid onto the must and stir until the sugar has dissolved. Cover.
2)   When the must has cooled to 22°C (70°F), add the other ingredients. Keep covered and ferment for 4 days, stirring 3 times daily.
3)   Strain the must into the fermenter, fit airlock and continue to ferment to dryness (SG about 1000).
4)   Rack when all bubbling has ceased. Top up and rack again as soon as the wine is really clear. Thereafter store at 10°C (50°F), rack and sulphite (½ tablet) every 3 months

until no more sediment appears. Bottle and store for another 6 months.

Rice wine *(strong white after-dinner wine)*

1400 g	rice	3 lb
450 g	washed raisins or sultanas	1 lb
1000 g	granulated sugar	2 lb 3 oz
	juice of 1 lemon	
2.5 ml	tartaric acid	½ tsp
2.5 ml	malic acid	½ tsp
5 ml	starch enzyme (Amylozyme etc)	1 tsp
3	vitamin B₁ tablets	
	super or Tokay yeast and nutrients	
	sulphite tablets	

1)   Prepare the yeast starter (see page 41). Chop or mince the raisins and place the puree with half the sugar in the mash-tun. Add 3 litres (5½ pts) of boiling water, stirring until the sugar has dissolved. Wash the rice in cold water and add it when the must has cooled to warm. Cover.
2)   Next day add the other ingredients except the rest of the sugar and stir. Ferment for 10 days at 22°C (70°F) stirring 3 times daily.
3)   Strain must through a fine sieve or nylon cloth into the fermenter and add 2 vitamin tablets. Ensure that must is only shoulder-high and top up if necessary, then fit airlock. When the ferment slows down (SG 1010), start feeding the remaining sugar in 113 g (4 oz) lots. Ferment to dryness.
4)   Rack at SG 1000 and top up with water. Rack again as soon as the wine is really clear and store at 10°C (50°F). Rack and sulphite (½ tablet) for every 3 months for a year, then bottle and store for another 6 months.

Pre-dinner cocktail: add 1 measure of gin to 3 measures of the apéritif wine. Serve with a cube of ice and a slice of lemon or orange peel

Rosehip wine (*medium rosé table wine*)

350 ml	rosehip syrup	12 oz
300 ml	white or rosé grape concentrate	½ pint
900 g	granulated sugar	2 lb
5 ml	grape tannin	1 tsp
5 ml	tartaric acid	1 tsp
2.5 ml	citric acid	½ tsp
5 ml	pectic enzyme	1 tsp
	Beaujolais or all-purpose yeast and nutrients	
	sulphite tablets	

1) Prepare the yeast starter (see page 41). Place all the ingredients except the yeast in the mash-tun. Add tap water to make must up to 4 litres (7 pints). Stir until the sugar has dissolved, add 2 crushed sulphite tablets and cover.
2) Next day add the yeast and stir vigorously. Cover and ferment for 3 days at 22°C (70°F). Stir once a day.
3) Pour must into the fermenter, fit airlock and continue the fermentation at the same temperature. Rack when the fermentation has stopped completely (SG 995). For a slightly sweeter wine, add 113 g (4 oz) sugar just before racking (SG 1005).
4) Rack for the 2nd time some 14 days later when the wine should be really clear. Top up. Store at 10°C (50°F), racking and sulphiting (½ tablet) every 3 months. Bottle after 11 months and store for 6 months.

Blending wine (*or medium white table wine*)

1 l	white grape concentrate	2 pints
900 g	bananas	2 lb
450 g	dried fruit (raisins, apples, apricots etc.)	1 lb
450 g	granulated sugar	1 lb
250 ml	white or yellow rose petals	½ pint
5 ml	tartaric acid	1 tsp
5 ml	citric acid	1 tsp
5 ml	pectic enzyme	1 tsp
3	vitamin B$_1$ tablets	
	Sauternes yeast and nutrients	
	sulphite tablets	

1) Make up yeast starter (see page 41). Chop or mince the dried fruit and place in mash-tun. Peel and slice the bananas (add the sliced peel of one) and boil the slices in 2 litres (3½ pts) of water for 20 minutes. Strain the hot banana juice into the mash-tun, add half the sugar and stir until dissolved. Make up the liquid must to just under 4 litres (7 pts) with sterile water. Cover.

2) When the must has cooled to 22°C (70°F), stir in the acids, nutrients, enzyme and yeast. Ferment on the pulp for 5 days stirring at least once per day.
3) Lightly press the pulp and strain the must into the fermenter; fit airlock. When the ferment slows down, add the rose petals and start sugar feeding (see page 29) the rest of the sugar.
4) Rack when fermentation is over – which may take a month or so. For a sweet wine, top up with 113 g (4 oz) sugar diluted in water (SG 1010) and add 2 sulphite tablets. Rack again when the wine is really clear. Store for 9 months at 10°C (50°F) racking and sulphiting (½ tablet) every 3 months. Bottle if there is no residue and store for another 6 months.

Fruit wines

The fruits most useful to winemakers become available in the autumn and the few weeks when they are in abundance are the occasion for concentrated winemaking. The late autumn is a good time for a 'wine-holiday' when perhaps the whole family helps with the main crop or with the picking and preparing of minor additions such as berries, herbs and flowers. The end of the fruit season is also the time when fruit farmers and grocers gladly sell in bulk at much lower prices and when fruit juices are being extracted at many fruit farms.

Juice extraction in bulk requires equipment which is too expensive for most amateurs, so the opportunity to obtain juice in this way should always be seized. Whenever a recipe calls for juice extraction, and it proves impossible to obtain any ready-made, check page 37 for an alternative method.

Fruit wines are usually rich in flavour and whilst they can achieve the same perfection as grape wines, different types of fruit produce a wide range of enjoyable tastes. Always select the ripest fruit available, although windfalls can be included as long as badly bruised and mildewed parts are removed. Remove the stones from fruit such as peaches but leave the pips of apples and grapes, as long as they are not being crushed.

Apple wine (*dry white table wine*)

2260 g	mixed apples (add a few crab apples if possible)	5 lb
340 g	granulated sugar	$\frac{3}{4}$ lb
600 ml	white grape concentrate	1 pint
400 ml	orange juice	$\frac{3}{4}$ pint
280 ml	fresh (or 14 g dried) elderflowers	$\frac{1}{2}$ pint
5 ml	grape tannin	1 tsp
5 ml	pectic enzyme	1 tsp
	Graves yeast and nutrients	
	sulphite tablets	

1) Prepare the yeast starter (see page 41). Press out the apple juice and pour into mash-tun, adding 2 sulphite tablets. Press sufficient oranges to obtain 400 ml ($\frac{3}{4}$ pt) juice (or buy it). Add it together with the enzyme and cover.
2) Next day, rack the clear juice off its pulp-deposit, add the other ingredients except the flowers and make up the must to 4 litres (7 pts) with cold sterile water. Ferment at 22°C (70°F) for 3 days, stirring twice daily.
3) Pour must into fermenter and fit airlock. After 5 days add the sterile flowers (see page 38) and ferment to dryness (SG 995–1000).
4) Rack and strain out the flowers and as soon as the wine is really clear, rack again and store at 10°C (50°F). Store in bulk for a total of 11 months, racking and sulphiting ($\frac{1}{2}$ tablet) every 3rd month. Store in bottle for another 6 months.

Apple wine (*dry red table wine*)

2700 g	mixed apples	6 lb
900 g	elderberries	2 lb
780 g	granulated sugar	$1\frac{3}{4}$ lb
600 ml	red grape concentrate	1 pint
10 ml	pectic enzyme	2 tsp
	Bordeaux yeast and nutrients	
	sulphite tablets	

1) Prepare the yeast starter (see page 41). Press the sliced apples and pour juice into mash-tun. Do not discard the pulp. Wash and crush the elderberries and add the strained juice to mash-tun. Pour 1 litre ($1\frac{1}{2}$ pts) of boiling water over the elderberry pulp, stir 5 minutes, then strain into tun. Combine the 2 pulps, soak them in 1 litre boiling water and stir for 5 minutes, strain and add together with 2 sulphite tablets. When cool, add the enzyme and cover.

2) Next day add the other ingredients, bring the must up to 4 litres (7 pts) and ferment for 5 days at 22°C (70°F).
3) Strain must into fermenter, fit airlock and ferment to dryness. Then rack and rack again as soon as the wine is really clear.
4) Store wine at 10°C (50°F), ideally in wood, for 2 years, racking and sulphiting ($\frac{1}{2}$ tablet) every 3rd month. Keep in bottle for at least another year.

Note: *a further 4.5 litres of rosé wine can be made from the apple and elderberry pulps used earlier. Place the pulp in the mash-tun and add 3 litres ($5\frac{1}{2}$ pts) of cold, sterile water. Add the same amount of grape concentrate and sugar but no yeast since the pulp contains enough to start a fresh ferment. Pulp ferment for 5 days then continue as from* 3).

Apple wine (*sweet white after-dinner wine*)

2700 g	mixed apples	6 lb
680 g	granulated sugar	$1\frac{1}{2}$ lb
400 ml	white grape concentrate	$\frac{3}{4}$ pint
300 ml	white or yellow rose petals	$\frac{1}{2}$ pint
2.5 ml	tartaric acid	$\frac{1}{2}$ tsp
2.5 ml	citric acid	$\frac{1}{2}$ tsp
2.5 ml	grape tannin	$\frac{1}{2}$ tsp
5 ml	pectic enzyme	1 tsp
	Sauternes yeast and nutrients	
	sulphite tablets	

1) Prepare the yeast starter (see page 41). Wash the apples in warm water then slice them (no need to core) and place in the mash-tun. Add 3 litres (5 pts) tap-water, the enzyme and acids, half the sugar and 2 sulphite tablets and stir until the sugar has dissolved. Cover.
2) Next day add the other ingredients except the flowers and bring the must up to 4.5 litres (8 pts) with sterile water. Ferment at 22°C (70°F) for 4 days, stirring 3 times daily.
3) Press the pulp hard but slowly and pour the juice into the fermenter. Fit airlock. After 8 days, feed the sulphited (see page 39) rose petals into the must. Whenever the ferment slows (SG about 1000), feed the rest of the sugar in 113 g (4 oz) proportions. Terminate fermentation when the airlock shows less than a bubble once a minute (SG 1010–1015) by racking and sulphiting (2 tablets).
4) Rack for the second time when the wine is really clear. Mature the wine in bulk for at least 12 months, racking and sulphiting ($\frac{1}{2}$ tablet) at 3-monthly intervals. Store in bottle for 6 months.

Apple sherry *(fino)*

1300 g	mixed apples	3	lb
1300 g	peeled bananas	3	lb
680 g	demerara sugar	1½	lb
400 ml	white grape concentrate	¾	pint
50 g	cream of tartar	2	oz
5 ml	pectic enzyme	1	tsp
3	vitamin B₁ tablets		
	Sherry yeast and nutrients		
	sulphite tablets		

1) Prepare the yeast starter (see page 41). Mince or mash the apples and press out the juice. Place in mash-tun together with half the sugar. Slice the bananas and boil for 20 minutes in 2 litres (3½ pts) of water. Strain juice into the mash-tun and stir until the sugar has dissolved. Add 2 sulphite tablets and cover.

2) Next day add the other ingredients but only 2 vitamin tablets and bring the must up to 4 litres (7 pts) with sterile water. Ferment for 4 days at 22°C (70°F), stirring once a day.

3) Pour must into fermenter, add 1 vitamin tablet and plug neck with cotton wool. Whenever ferment slows, add 113 g (4 oz) sugar and ferment to dryness (SG 995–1000).

4) Rack but do not top up and keep vessel plugged with cotton wool. Do not worry if surface develops a white film, the 'sherry flor'. Keep for 2 years, then carefully rack and bottle.

Banana wine *(sweet white 'Sauternes' style)*

1800 g	very ripe peeled bananas	4	lb
450 g	granulated sugar	1	lb
600 ml	white grape concentrate	1	pint
400 ml	yellow rose petals	¾	pint
42 ml	Glycerol	1½	fl oz
5 ml	tartaric acid	1	tsp
2.5 ml	citric acid	½	tsp
2.5 ml	malic acid	½	tsp
5 ml	pectic enzyme	1	tsp
2.5 ml	grape tannin	½	tsp
	Sauternes yeast and nutrients		
	sulphite tablets		

1) Prepare the yeast starter (see page 41). Slice the bananas and boil them for 20 minutes in a saucepan. Place half the sugar in the mash-tun and pour over it the hot, strained banana juice. Add the grape concentrate and the acids and make up the must to 4 litres (7 pts). Add 1 crushed sulphite tablet, cover and let cool.

2) Next day add the other ingredients except the rest of the sugar and ferment the must at 22°C (70°F) for 4 days, stirring twice daily.

3) Pour the must into the fermenter, fit airlock and when the ferment slows, sugar-feed the rest of the sugar in 113 g (4 oz) portions. Add the last quantity just before racking (SG about 1010).

4) Rack and add 2 sulphite tablets. Rack again, about 2–3 weeks later when the wine should be really clear, and top up. Store in bulk at 10°C (50°F) for 2 years, racking and sulphiting (½ tablet) every 3 months. Bottle and keep for another year.

Cherry wine *(dry red table wine)*

3600 g	mixed cherries	8	lb
900 g	sultanas or raisins	2	lb
300 g	granulated sugar	¾	lb
400 ml	red rose petals	¾	pint
5 ml	grape tannin	1	tsp
5 ml	pectic enzyme	1	tsp
	Burgundy yeast and nutrients		
	sulphite tablets		

1) Prepare the yeast starter (see page 41). Wash, stone and crush the cherries and place them with the minced sultanas in the mash-tun. Add 2 litres (3½ pts) of tap-water and the sugar and stir until it has dissolved. Add 2 sulphite tablets and cover.

2) Next day stir in the rest of the ingredients except the flowers and make the must up to 4 litres (7 pts). Ferment on the pulp at 22°C (70°F) until a deep red colour is obtained (about 5–8 days).

3) Press the pulp in a nylon bag and strain the juice into the fermenter. Fit airlock. After three days, add the sterilised rose petals (see page 38). Ferment to dryness and rack.

4) About 3 weeks later, when the wine is really clear, rack again and top up. Mature in wood if possible for 1 year, racking and sulphiting (½ tablet) every 3 months then store in bottle for 2 more years.

Cherry wine (sweet, light red, after-dinner wine)

2000 g	mixed cooking and Morello cherries	4½	lb
1250 g	demerara or white sugar	2¾	lb
600 ml	red grape concentrate	1	pint
5 ml	tartaric acid	1	tsp
5 ml	citric acid	1	tsp
5 ml	pectic enzyme	1	tsp
	Bordeaux yeast and nutrients		
	sulphite tablets		

1) Make up the yeast starter (see page 41). Wash, stone and crush the cherries and place them in the mash-tun. Add 2 litres (3½ pts) of tap-water, the pectic enzyme, and 1 sulphite tablet. Stir and cover.
2) Next day add the other ingredients but only 500 g (1 lb) of the sugar and make up the must to 4 litres (7 pts) with sterile water. Ferment on the pulp for 5 days at 22°C (70°F) and stir at least 3 times daily.
3) Press out the juice in a nylon bag and strain it into the fermenter. Fit airlock. When the ferment slows, sugar-feed the rest of the sugar in 113 g (4 oz) portions, adding the last portion before racking (SG about 1015).
4) Rack and add 2 sulphite tablets to terminate fermentation. Rack again and top up as soon as the wine is really clear. Mature in bulk (and ideally in wood) for at least a year, racking and sulphiting (½ tablet) at 3-monthly intervals. Store in bottle for a further 12 months at least.

Gooseberry wine (light dry white table wine)

2260 g	topped and tailed ripe gooseberries	5	lb
450 g	honey	1	lb
600 ml	white grape concentrate	1	pint
226 g	granulated sugar	½	lb
300 ml	white or yellow rose petals	½	pint
5 ml	pectic enzyme	1	tsp
	Hock yeast and nutrients		
	sulphite tablets		

1) Prepare the yeast starter (see page 41). Crush the gooseberries and place them with the honey in the mash-tun. Pour 2 litres (3½ pts) boiling water over the pulp and stir until the honey has dissolved. When cool, add the enzyme, yeast and nutrients and ferment on the pulp for 4 days at 22°C (70°F).
2) Press the must in a nylon bag and strain the liquid into the fermenter. Add the grape concentrate and top up to shoulder-high. Fit airlock.

3) After 5 days, sterilise the flowers (see page 38) and add them to the must. When the ferment slows, feed the sugar in 113 g (4 oz) portions. Ferment to dryness.
4) Rack at SG 1000, strain out the petals and rack again when the wine is really clear. Store at 10°C (50°F) for 9 months, racking and sulphiting (½ tablet) every 3rd month. Bottle and store for 6 months.

Gooseberry wine (*sweet white dessert wine*)

3175 g	overripe gooseberries	7	lb
450 g	sultanas or raisins	1	lb
900 g	granulated sugar	2	lb
280 ml	white grape concentrate	½	pint
450 ml	white or yellow rose petals	¾	pint
50 ml	Glycerol	1½	fl oz
1	vitamin B₁ tablet		
5 ml	tartaric acid	1	tsp
5 ml	citric acid	1	tsp
5 ml	pectic enzyme	1	tsp
	Sauternes yeast and nutrients		
	sulphite tablets		

1) Prepare the yeast starter (see page 41). Wash and crush the gooseberries, mince the sultanas and stir in half the sugar until dissolved. Add the grape concentrate, enzyme and 2 sulphite tablets and make up the must with tap-water to 4 litres (7 pts). Cover.
2) Next day add the other ingredients except half of the sugar and ferment at 22°C (70°F) for 3 days, stirring 3 times daily.
3) Press the pulp lightly and strain the liquor into the fermenter. Fit air lock. After 5 days, add the sterilised petals (see page 38). When the ferment slows (SG 1005), feed the rest of the sugar in 113 g (4 oz) quantities, adding the last portion just before racking (SG 1015).
4) Rack, strain out the petals and add 2 sulphite tablets. Rack again when the wine is really clear. Store at 10°C (50°F) for 2 years, racking and sulphiting (½ tablet) every 3 months. Store in bottle for another year.

Damson wine (*sweet red dessert wine*)

2200 g	ripe damsons	5	lb
340 g	sultanas	¾	lb
450 g	demerara sugar	1	lb
450 g	white granulated sugar	1	lb
500 g	peeled bananas	1	lb
300 ml	red grape concentrate	½	pint
10 ml	pectic enzyme	2	tsp
5 ml	tartaric acid	1	tsp
5 ml	citric acid	1	tsp
	super or port yeast and nutrients		
	sulphite tablets		

1) Prepare the yeast starter (see page 41). Wash, stone and crush the damsons in the mash-tun. Add the minced sultanas, grape concentrate and half the sugar. Slice the bananas and boil them for 20 minutes in 2 litres (3½ pts) of water and add the strained liquor. Make up the must to 4.5 litres (8 pts), add 2 sulphite tablets and let cool.
2) Next day, add the other ingredients except the rest of the sugar and ferment on the pulp at 22°C (70°F) for 5 days, stirring 3 times daily.
3) Strain and press the must and pour the liquid into the fermenter. Fit airlock. When the ferment slows (2–3 weeks), stir in the remaining sugar in 113 g (4 oz) batches, feeding the last quantity just before racking (SG 1010–1015).
4) Rack and add 2 sulphite tablets. Rack again when the wine is really clear (NB – it takes longer than usual with damsons) and top up. Store for 2 years in bulk, racking and sulphiting (½ tablet) every 3 months. Try and be patient and keep the bottles for 2 years before drinking.

Damson wine *(sweet port-wine style)*

2260 g	ripe damsons	5	lb
450 g	elderberries	1	lb
900 g	sultanas or raisins	2	lb
900 g	ripe peeled bananas	2	lb
450 g	demerara sugar	1	lb
100 ml	brandy or vodka	3	fl oz
5 ml	pectic enzyme	1	tsp
5 ml	grape tannin	1	tsp
5 ml	tartaric acid	1	tsp
3	vitamin B_1 tablets		
	super or Tokay yeast and nutrients		
	sulphite tablets		

1) Prepare the yeast starter (see page 41). Wash, stone and crush the damsons in the mash-tun. Crush and strain the elderberries and add their juice (using the pulp for other wine – see page 72). Add the washed and minced sultanas. Boil the sliced bananas in 2 litres (3½ pts) of water and add the strained juice, making the must up to 4.5 litres (8 pts). Add 2 sulphite tablets and cover.
2) The next day add the other ingredients except the sugar and brandy and ferment on the pulp at 22°C (70°F) for 5 days, stirring 3 times daily to break up the cap.
3) Press the pulp in a nylon bag (wearing rubber gloves) and pour the clear liquor into the fermenter. Fit airlock. Sugar-feed the sugar and ferment to SG about 1020, then rack.
4) Rack again when the wine is really clear and top up. Rack again 3 months later and add the brandy. Store in bulk for at least 2 years, ideally in wood, racking and sulphiting (½ tablet) at 3-monthly intervals. Store the bottles for 2 years.

Plum wine *(medium white table or social wine)*

2260 g	ripe plums or greengages	5	lb
1350 g	granulated sugar	3	lb
300 ml	white grape concentrate	½	pint
10 ml	pectic enzyme	2	tsp
5 ml	tartaric acid	1	tsp
	Bordeaux yeast and nutrients		
	sulphite tablets		

1) Prepare the yeast starter (see page 41). Wash, stone and crush the plums in the mash-tun. Add the enzyme, 1 sulphite tablet, and 2 litres (3½ pts) of tap-water, and stir in half the sugar until it has dissolved. Cover.
2) Next day, add the other ingredients and make the must up to 4.5 litres (8 pts) and ferment on the pulp at 22°C (70°F) for 5 days, stirring 3 times daily.

3) Press the pulp gently and strain the liquor into the fermenter. Fit airlock. Towards the end of the fermentation, stir in the rest of the sugar in 113 g (4 oz) quantities.
4) Rack just after the last portion of sugar has been added (SG 1010) and rack again when the wine is really clear (NB – with plums this may take longer than usual). Store at 10°C (50°F) for 1 year and another year in the bottle.

Sloe wine *(medium red table-wine)*

900 g	ripe sloes	2	lb
560 g	honey (or 450 g sugar)	1¼	lb
560 ml	red grape concentrate	1	pint
560 ml	red rose petals	1	pint
5 ml	pectic enzyme	1	tsp
5 ml	tartaric acid	1	tsp
	Burgundy yeast and nutrients		
	sulphite tablets		

1) Prepare the yeast starter (see page 41). Crush and stone the sloes, add the enzyme, 1 crushed sulphite tablet and 2 litres (3½ pts) of tap-water. Cover.
2) Next day add the other ingredients except the flowers and only half the honey, make up the must to 4.5 litres (8 pts) and ferment on the pulp at 22°C (70°F) for 4 days, stirring 3 times daily.
3) When the must is a deep red colour, press the pulp lightly and strain the juice into the fermenter. Fit airlock. After 5 days sterilise the rose petals (see page 38) and feed them into the fermenter. When the ferment slows, add the rest of the honey in 113 g (4 oz) portions, the last amount just before racking (SG 1010).
4) Rack and strain out the petals and after a few weeks, when the wine is really clear, rack again and top up. Mature in wood if possible for 1 year, racking every 3 months, and store at 10°C (50°F). Since this wine matures slowly, store in bottle for 2 years.

Peach wine *(dry white table wine)*

1800 g	ripe peaches or apricots	4 lb
900 g	granulated sugar	2 lb
280 ml	white grape concentrate	$\frac{1}{2}$ pint
280 ml	white or yellow rose petals	$\frac{1}{2}$ pint
2.5 ml	tartaric acid	$\frac{1}{2}$ tsp
2.5 ml	citric acid	$\frac{1}{2}$ tsp
5 ml	grape tannin	1 tsp
5 ml	pectic enzyme	1 tsp
	Chablis yeast and nutrients	
	sulphite tablets	

1) Prepare the yeast starter (see page 41). Stone and crush the peaches and press out the juice in a nylon bag. Make up with tap-water to 3 litres (5½ pts). Add 2 sulphite tablets and allow to settle.
2) Next day, rack the juice off the pulp. Make a sugar-syrup (900 g sugar in 1 litre boiling water) and add. When cool, add the other ingredients except the flowers and ferment for 2 days at 22°C (70°F).
3) Pour must into fermentation jar, add the petals 5 days later and rack when fermentation has ceased, straining out the petals. Rack again when the wine is really clear. Store in bulk at 10°C (50°F) for 9 months before bottling, racking every 3 months. Store for 6 months in bottle.

Peach wine *(medium white after-dinner wine)*

3600 g	ripe peaches or apricots	8 lb
900 g	ripe bananas	2 lb
570 g	honey	$1\frac{1}{4}$ lb
450 g	granulated sugar	1 lb
280 ml	light-coloured rose petals	$\frac{1}{2}$ pint
5 ml	grape tannin	1 tsp
5 ml	tartaric acid	1 tsp
5 ml	pectic enzyme	1 tsp
	super or Madeira yeast and nutrients	
	sulphite tablets	

1) Prepare the yeast starter (see page 41). Stone the peaches and press out the juice in a nylon bag. Add 2 litres (3½ pts) tap-water, 2 sulphite tablets, cover and allow to settle.
2) Next day, slice the bananas with their skins and boil for 20 minutes in 2 litres (3½ pts) of water. Syphon the peach juice off the lees and place in mash-tun with the honey. Pour on the hot banana juice and stir until the honey has dissolved. When cool, stir in the other in-gredients except the sugar, make up the must to 4 litres (7 pts) and ferment at 22°C (70°F) for 3 days.
3) Pour must into fermenter and fit airlock. Add the sterile flower petals (see page 38) 8 days later. When the ferment slows, add the granulated sugar in 113 g (4 oz) portions, the last one just before racking (SG 1015).
4) Rack, strain out the petals and add 2 sulphite tablets. Rack again when the wine is really clear. Store in bulk at about 10°C (50°F) for at least 2 years, racking and sulphiting (½ tablet) every 3rd month. Bottle and store for 6 months.

Grape wine *(red dry table wine)*

5.5–7 kg	fresh ripe black grapes	12–15 lb
600 g	granulated sugar	$1\frac{1}{4}$ lb
	Burgundy yeast and nutrients	
	sulphite tablets	

Collect the grapes when they are ripe, or even over-ripe, and mash them the same day. Discard any damaged or mouldy grapes, remove the main (greenish-yellow) stalks but leave the short (pink) stalks. Collect enough grapes to produce 5 litres (just over 1 gal) of must. Grapes collected after a normal summer in the 30–40° latitudes should need no sugar but those grown in the 40–50° latitudes, with their cooler climate, need the sugar suggested in the recipe (a strained sample of must should have a SG of about 1085).
1) Prepare the yeast starter (see page 41). Crush the grapes with your hands and place the juice, skins and pips in the mash-tun. Add the sugar, if required, to the must and stir until it has dissolved. Add 2 crushed sulphite tablets and cover.
2) Next day add the yeast starter. Once the must is fermenting it will tend to push up the pulp so place a heavy float such as a weighted plate on the must to keep the pulpy cap submerged. Cover and ferment on the pulp at 22°C (70°F) for 10 days to achieve a light red colour and up to 14 days for a deeper colour. Stir the must twice a day.
3) Press the pulp hard in a nylon bag and strain the juice into the fermenter, fit airlock and ferment to dryness (SG 995). Rack into clean vessel.
4) Rack again after 2-3 weeks when the wine should be clear and store at 10°C (50°F) away from light. Store in bulk for at least 2 years (ideally in wood) racking and sulphiting (½ tablet) every 3 months. Store in bottle for another year before serving.

Grape wine *(dry white table wine)*

5.5–7 kg	ripe fresh white or black grapes	12–15 lb
600 g	granulated sugar	1¼ lb
	Hock yeast and nutrients	
	sulphite tablets	

Collect the grapes and consider sugaring as described for red grape wine.

1) Prepare the yeast starter (see page 41). Discard any unsound grapes and remove all stalks. Extract the juice in a press or crush the grapes and squeeze their juice out by hand with a nylon bag. Place juice in mash-tun, add sugar if needed (a sample of the must should have SG about 1080), add 2 sulphite tablets and cover.

2) Next day add the yeast and nutrients and ferment at 22°C (70°F) for 2 days. Then pour must into fermenter, fit airlock and ferment to dryness (SG 995).

3) Rack into clean vessel, top up and rack again when the wine is really clear. Store at 10°C (50°F).

4) Mature in wood or glass for a year, racking and sulphiting (½ tablet) every 3rd month. Keep in bottle for another 6 months.

Grape sherry *(medium)*

450 g	ripe white grapes	1 lb
450 g	sultanas or raisins	1 lb
225 g	overripe peeled bananas	½ lb
225 g	peeled and sliced potatoes	½ lb
560 g	demerara sugar	1¼ lb
14 g	cream of tartar	½ oz
10 ml	pectic enzyme	1 tsp
3	vitamin B_1 tablets	
	Sherry yeast and nutrients	
	sulphite tablets	

1) Make up the yeast starter (see page 41). Boil the sliced bananas in 2 litres (3½ pts) of water for 20 minutes. Meanwhile place the crushed grapes, minced sultanas and sliced potatoes in the mash-tun. Strain in the hot banana juice and stir well. Cover and when cool, add the enzyme, 2 sulphite tablets and make the must up to 4.5 litres (8 pts).

2) Next day add the other ingredients except the sugar and ferment the must at 22°C (70°F) for 4 days, stirring 3 times daily.

3) Lightly press the pulp and strain the liquor into the fermenter. Fit airlock. Whenever the ferment slows (SG 1000), add the sugar in 113 g (4 oz) portions, adding the last quantity just before racking, to finish with SG of about 1020.

4) Rack but do not top up and plug the neck of the fermenter with cotton wool so that air can reach the wine. Do not rack again since the yeast should develop a surface film called 'flor' which helps to produce the characteristic flavour of sherry. Do not disturb for 2 years, then carefully rack (1 sulphite tablet) and bottle. Mature in bottle for another year at least.

Wines from berries

Berries contain more complex minerals and vitamins than fruit – ingredients that are very useful during fermentation but especially valuable in bringing about the slow changes in quality during maturing. Red wines made from berries generally need to mature for longer periods than wines made from other fruit and if you have the patience to wait, they will reward you with a quality equal to that of the best Burgundies and Clarets.

Ideally, wines made from red berries should mature in casks of more than 40 litres capacity, but since few amateurs have room for casks of this size, careful use of smaller casks is advised. To prevent over-oxidisation in small casks, store wine in them only for short periods and a practical routine is: 3 months in wood, rack; 3 months in glass, rack; and so on. Red wines stored in glass will be perfectly all right if racked every 3 months (so that they absorb some oxygen) but unfortunately they cannot attain the superb quality of wines which have matured in wood.

After being stored in bulk for 2 years, another 2 years in the bottle is the minimum period required for finishing these wines but, of course, every extra year improves their bouquet and flavour.

Bilberry or Blackberry wine (strong red port-style)

2720 g	bilberries (or blackberries)	6 lb
680 g	peeled bananas	1½ lb
450 g	sultanas or raisins	1 lb
850 ml	red grape concentrate	1½ pints
570 ml	red rose petals	1 pint
900 g (at least)	granulated sugar	1½ lb (minimum)
2.5 ml	grape tannin	½ tsp
2.5 ml	tartaric acid	½ tsp
5 ml	pectic enzyme	1 tsp
2	vitamin B$_1$ tablets	
	super or Madeira yeast and nutrients	
	sulphite tablets	

1) Prepare the yeast starter (see page 41). Wash the berries and crush them with a wooden spoon in the mash-tun. Add half the sugar. Slice the bananas, boil them for 20 minutes in 2 litres (3½ pts) of water and pour the hot juice into the mash-tun. Stir until the sugar has dissolved. When cool, add the concentrate, enzyme, tannin, acids, nutrients and yeast. Bring the must up to 4.5 litres (8 pts) and cover. Ferment at 22°C (70°F) for 5 days, stirring 3 times daily.
2) Press the must and strain juice into fermenter, add the vitamin tablets and fit airlock. Introduce the flowers (see page 38) after 5 days. Whenever the ferment slows down, feed the sugar in 113 g (4 oz) doses and add more if the ferment will allow it, adding the last dose before racking (SG 1020).
3) Rack and add 2 sulphite tablets. Rack again when the wine is really clear, top up and include up to 280 ml (½ pt) of cheap brandy. Store at 10°C (50°F), preferably in wood, for 2 years (racking every 3 months) and another 2 years at least in bottle.

Blackberry, Loganberry or Raspberry wine
(red medium table wine)

1800 g	berries	4 lb
226 g	ripe peeled bananas	½ lb
900 g	granulated sugar	2 lb
560 ml	red grape concentrate	1 pint
5 ml	grape tannin	1 tsp
2.5 ml	tartaric acid	½ tsp
5 ml	pectic enzyme	1 tsp
	Bordeaux yeast and nutrients	
	sulphite tablets	

1) Prepare the yeast starter (see page 41). Slice the bananas and boil them in 2 litres (3½ pts) of water for 20 minutes. Meanwhile crush the berries in the mash-tun

and add the sugar. Strain the hot banana juice onto the sugar and stir until it has dissolved. Add 1 sulphite tablet and cover.
2) Next day, add the rest of the ingredients and make up the must to 4 litres (7 pts). Ferment at 22°C (70°F) for 5 days, then strain into the fermenter, pressing the pulp.
3) Rack when fermentation is over. Rack again as soon as the wine is really clear. Store at 10°C (50°F) for at least a year, racking and sulphiting (½ tablet) every 3 months. Keep another 6 months in bottle.

Elderberry wine (sweet red social wine)

900 g	elderberries	2 lb
680 g	bilberries, blackberries or sloes	1½ lb
450 g	sultanas or raisins	1 lb
780 g	granulated sugar	1½ lb
600 ml	red rose petals	1 pint
5 ml	grape tannin	1 tsp
5 ml	pectic enzyme	1 tsp
2	vitamin B$_1$ tablets	
	super or Madeira yeast and nutrients	
	sulphite tablets	

1) Prepare the yeast starter (see page 41). Crush the elderberries and bilberries in a saucepan and pour 1 litre (1½ pts) boiling water over them. Strain juice into mash-tun and repeat. Add the minced sultanas, half the sugar and cover.
2) Next day, add the other ingredients except the flowers and half the sugar, make up the must to 4 litres (7 pts) and ferment at 22°C (70°F) for 4 days, stirring 3 times daily.
3) Press the pulp lightly and strain the juice into the fermenter. Retain the pulp and see recipe page 63. After 7 days, add the sterile petals (see page 38) and whenever the ferment slows, feed the sugar in 113 g (4 oz) portions, adding the last amount just before racking (SG 1015).
4) Rack and add 1 sulphite tablet. Rack again as soon as the wine is really clear. Store at 10°C (50°F) for at least 2 years, racking and sulphiting (½ tablet) every 3-4 months. Store in bottle for another year.

Elderberry wine (dry red table wine)

900 g	elderberries (or pulp left over from the recipe page 67)	2	lb
675 g	sloes or blackberries	1½	lb
560 g	granulated sugar	1¼	lb
280 ml	red grape concentrate	½	pint
550 ml	red rose petals or elderflowers	1	pint
5 ml	tartaric acid	1	tsp
5 ml	pectic enzyme	1	tsp
2	vitamin B₁ tablets		
	Bordeaux yeast and nutrients		
	sulphite tablets		

1) Prepare the yeast starter (see page 41). Wearing rubber gloves crush the sloes by hand, then crush the elderberries, add the sugar and pour 2 litres (3½ pts) boiling water over the pulp, stirring until the sugar has dissolved. Add 1 sulphite tablet, cover and cool.

2) Next day, add the other ingredients except the petals, make the must up to 4 litres (7 pts) and ferment on the pulp at 22°C (70°F) for 4 days, stirring 3 times daily.

3) Press the pulp lightly and strain the juice into the fermenter. Fit airlock. On the 7th day, add the sterilised flower petals and ferment almost to dryness (SG 995–1000).

4) Rack and strain out the petals. Rack again as soon as the wine is really clear. Store at 10°C (50°F) for a year, racking and sulphiting every 3rd month. Store in bottle for 6 months longer.

Elderberry wine (strong red port-style)

1360 g	elderberries (stalked with a fork)	3	lb
450 g	sultanas or damsons	1	lb
450 g	peeled bananas	1	lb
680 g	honey (or 450 g sugar)	1½	lb
5 ml	tartaric acid	1	tsp
5 ml	pectic enzyme	1	tsp
1	vitamin B₁ tablet		
	Madeira or Tokay yeast and nutrients		
	sulphite tablets		

1) Prepare the yeast starter (see page 41). Slice and boil the bananas in 1 litre (1½ pts) of water for 20 minutes. Crush the elderberries and pour the hot banana juice onto them. Strain the juice into the mash-tun. Pour another litre of hot water over the pulp, strain and add. Mince the sultanas and place the puree in the mash-tun. Add 2 sulphite tablets and cover.

2) Next day, add the other ingredients except the honey, make up the must to 4.5 litres (8 pts) and ferment on the pulp at 22°C (70°F). After 3 days, strain the must into the fermenter and press the pulp (wearing rubber gloves). Fit airlock and ferment until the bubble action slows down. Feed the honey in 113 g (4 oz) quantities but add more honey or sugar than stated if the yeast accepts it.

3) Rack just after the last addition of honey/sugar (SG 1020–1025) and add 2 sulphite tablets. Rack again, when the wine is really clear and top up. Since the wine will have about 17% alcohol, you might add 280 ml (½ pt) of cheap brandy to raise the alcohol level to about 20%. Rack at 3-monthly intervals, storing the wine at 10°C (50°F) for 2 years. Keep in bottle for another year at least.

Since flowers contribute only bouquet to a wine, body, flavour and alcohol have to be obtained from other ingredients. Because of their strong aroma, flower wines should be medium sweet – neither dry and thin, nor sickly sweet. Flower wine that is intended for blending however, may be sweeter than wine made for drinking. An addition of lactose will help retain sweetness in the finished wine.

Herbs, on the other hand, usually have a pronounced flavour and are therefore ideal for apéritif and after-dinner wines, although they too need extra ingredients to produce vinosity and alcohol. In some, lactose will again help to retain sweetness during fermentation.

Rose petal wine
(medium rosé or white, after-dinner or blending)

2.25 l	red, mixed or white rose petals, strongly scented	4	pints
900 ml	red or white grape concentrate	1½	pints
680 g	granulated sugar	1½	lb
40 g	lactose	1½	oz
2.5 ml	citric acid	½	tsp
2.5 ml	malic acid	½	tsp
5 ml	grape tannin	1	tsp
5 ml	pectic enzyme	1	tsp
	Sauternes yeast and nutrients		
	sulphite tablets		

1) Prepare the yeast starter (see page 41). Place the rose petals in the mash-tun. Add half the sugar, 2 litres (3½ pts) cold tap-water and stir until the sugar has dissolved. Add 1 sulphite tablet, and the acids and cover.
2) Next day, add the other ingredients except the remaining sugar, increase the must to 3.5 litres (6 pts) and ferment at 22°C (70°F) for 5 days, stirring twice daily.
3) Dissolve the remaining sugar in 250 ml (1 pt) boiling water, let cool and place in fermenter. Press the petals and strain the must into the fermenter. Shake until must and liquid sugar have combined. Fit airlock and ferment until there is a bubble only every minute (SG about 1010).
4) Rack and add 1 sulphite tablet. Rack again when the wine is really clear. Store at 10°C (50°F) for a year, racking and sulphiting (½ tablet) every 3 months. Keep in bottle for another 6 months.

Elderflower wine *(medium white after-dinner or blending)*

500 ml	elderflowers	¾	pint
250 ml	white grape concentrate	8	fl oz
900 g	sultanas or raisins	2	lb
670 g	granulated sugar	1½	lb
2.5 ml	citric acid	½	tsp
2.5 ml	tartaric acid	½	tsp
5 ml	pectic enzyme	1	tsp
5 ml	grape tannin	1	tsp
	Sauternes yeast and nutrients		
	sulphite tablets		

1) Prepare the yeast starter (see page 41). Use scissors to cut the flowers off their stems and place them in the mash-tun. Mince the sultanas and place the puree in a saucepan, add half the sugar and pour 2 litres (3½ pts) boiling water over the pulp. Stir until the sugar has dissolved. When cool, pour the pulp into the mash-tun, add the concentrate and the acids and make up the must to 4 litres (7 pts). Add 1 sulphite tablet and cover.
2) Next day add the other ingredients, except the remaining sugar, and ferment at 22°C (70°F) for 5 days, stirring 3 times daily.
3) Press the pulp lightly and strain the liquor into the fermenter. Fit airlock. Add the rest of the sugar in 113 g (4 oz) lots whenever the ferment slows, the last one shortly before racking (SG about 1010).
4) Rack and add 1 sulphite tablet. Rack again when the wine is really clear. Store for a year in bulk at 10°C (50°F), racking and sulphiting (½ tablet) every 3 months. Keep in bottle for 6 months before drinking or blending.

Tea wine (*dry white table or blending wine*)

90 ml	strongly scented China or Indian tea	3 fl oz or 6 tbs
600 ml	white grape concentrate	1 pint
900 g	granulated sugar	2 lb
2.5 ml	each tartaric, citric and malic acids	½ tsp
	Tokay yeast and nutrients	
	sulphite tablets	

1) Prepare the yeast starter (see page 41). Pour 1 litre (1½ pts) of boiling water over 5 tbs of the tea in a saucepan and let it infuse until cool. Pour 1 litre (1½ pts) boiling water over the sugar in the mash-tun and stir until dissolved. Combine the two liquids, straining the tea, add 1 sulphite tablet and cover.

2) Next day add the other ingredients, add the 6th spoon of tea and make up the must to 4 litres (7 pts). Cover and ferment for 2 days at 22°C (70°F).

3) Strain the must into the fermenter, fit airlock and ferment almost to dryness (SG 1000–1005).

4) Rack and sulphite (1 tablet) and rack again when the wine is really clear. Rack 3 times more before bottling and keep in bottle 6 months before drinking or blending.

Ginger wine (*medium white after-dinner wine*)

125 g	root ginger	4 oz
450 g	sultanas or raisins	1 lb
675 g	very ripe, peeled bananas	1½ lb
900 g	granulated sugar	2 lb
5 ml	each tartaric and citric acid	1 tsp
5 ml	grape tannin	1 tsp
5 ml	pectic enzyme	1 tsp
1	vitamin B₁ tablet	
	Sauternes yeast and nutrients	
	sulphite tablets	

1) Prepare yeast starter (see page 41). Slice the bananas and boil them in 3 litres (5½ pts) of water for 20 minutes. Meanwhile mince the sultanas, break up the ginger, bruise the pieces and place in the mash-tun with the sultanas and half the sugar. Strain in the hot banana liquor and stir until the sugar has dissolved. Cover and let cool.

2) Next day, add the other ingredients except the remaining sugar, make up the must to 4.5 litres (8 pts) and ferment on the pulp for 6 days at 22°C (70°F), stirring 3 times daily.

3) Press and strain out the solids, pouring the juice into the fermenter. Fit airlock. Whenever the ferment slows, feed the remaining sugar in 113 g (4 oz) portions, adding the last quantity a few days before the ferment is finished (SG 1010).

4) Rack and add 1 sulphite tablet. Rack again when the wine is really clear. Taste it for flavour and consider adding other herbs or spices to make it into an apéritif wine (see page 39). Store at 10°C (50°F) for at least a year, racking and sulphiting (½ tablet) at 3 monthly intervals. Store in bottle for 6 months.

Balm, Mint, Parsley or Thyme wine
(*medium white table or apéritif wine*)

	2.5 l	balm tips	4 pints
or	900 ml	mint leaves	1½ pints
or	1.2 l	parsley leaves (no stalks)	2 pints
or	1.2 l	lemon thyme (no stalks)	2 pints
	225 g	sultanas or raisins	½ lb
	1130 g	granulated sugar	2½ lb
or	1360 g	honey	3 lb
	14 g	root ginger	½ oz
	2.5 ml	each of citric, malic and tartaric acid	½ tsp
	5 ml	grape tannin	1 tsp
	5 ml	pectic enzyme	1 tsp
		Chablis yeast and nutrients	
		sulphite tablets	

1) Prepare the yeast starter (see page 41). Bruise leaves and ginger and cover in a saucepan with 2 litres (3½ pts) boiling water. Let it infuse for 24 hours.

2) Place half the sugar and the minced sultanas in the mash-tun, add 2 litres (3½ pts) boiling water and stir until the sugar has dissolved. Add the pressed and strained herb liquor, the other ingredients (except the rest of the sugar) and ferment at 22°C (70°F) for 4 days, stirring 3 times daily.

3) Press the pulp lightly and strain the liquid into the fermenter. Fit airlock. Whenever the ferment slows, feed the rest of the sugar in 113 g (4 oz) portions, adding the last amount shortly before racking (SG 1005–1010).

4) Rack and sulphite (2 tablets) and when the wine is really clear, rack again. At this stage you may want to try out other taste-combinations by adding herbs or essences (see page 39) to make different types of apéritif wine.

5) Rack and sulphite (2 tablets) once more. Store in bulk at 10°C (50°F), racking and lightly sulphiting every 3 months. Bottle after 11 months and keep the bottles 6 months before serving.

Vegetable wines

Vegetable wines will not easily attain the flavour of fruit wines but they will allow you to make reasonable wines when fruit or berries are not in season. Vegetable wines are often bland but they are useful for blending with sharper or more aromatic wines as they provide body.

The vegetables most commonly used for winemaking are parsnips, followed by beetroot and carrots. Parsnips are best taken from the ground after a short hard frost; beetroot and carrot in the autumn, when they are fully ripe.

Vegetables, like bananas, have to be boiled to give up their liquor, a process which extracts starch as well as pectin and enzymes for both have to be added to prevent hazes in the finished wines.

Parsnip wine *(dry white table wine)*

1585 g	washed and scrubbed parsnips	3½	lb
900 g	granulated sugar	2	lb
450 ml	unsweetened lemon or orange juice	¾	pint
300 ml	white grape concentrate	½	pint
14 g	dried elderflowers	½	oz
5 ml	tartaric acid	1	tsp
5 ml	grape tannin	1	tsp
5 ml	pectic enzyme	1	tsp
2.5 ml	starch enzyme	½	tsp
	Graves yeast and nutrients		
	sulphite tablets		

1) Prepare the yeast starter (see page 41). Slice the parsnips and boil them in a saucepan in 2.5 litres (4½ pts) of water until tender (about 20 mins). Place the sugar in the mash-tun then, pressing the pulp lightly, strain the hot juice over the sugar. Stir until the sugar has dissolved. Add the orange or lemon juice and 1 sulphite tablet, cover and let cool.
2) Next day add the other ingredients except the flowers, make up the must to 4 litres (7 pts) and ferment for 8 days at 22° C (70°F) stirring daily.
3) Pour must into the fermenter and fit airlock. After 3 days introduce the flowers and ferment until there is a bubble only once every minute (SG 1000–1005).
4) Rack, strain out the flowers and add 1 sulphite tablet. Rack again as soon as the wine is really clear. Store in bulk for 10 months at 10°C (50°F), racking and sulphiting (½ tablet) every 3 months. Store in bottle for 6 months.

Parsnip wine *(sweet white after-dinner or blending wine)*

1360 g	washed and scrubbed parsnips	3	lb
900 g	honey	2	lb
600 ml	white grape concentrate	1	pint
14 g	dried elderflowers	½	oz
42 ml	Glycerol	1½	fl oz
5 ml	each citric, tartaric and malic acid	3	tsp in all
5 ml	grape tannin	1	tsp
5 ml	pectic enzyme	1	tsp
2.5 ml	starch enzyme	½	tsp
	Sauternes yeast and nutrients		
	sulphite tablets		

1) Prepare the yeast starter (see page 41). Dice the parsnips and boil in a large saucepan for 30 minutes in 3 litres (5½ pts) of water. Place half the honey in the mash-tun and dissolve it with the hot strained parsnip juice. Add 1 sulphite tablet, cover and let cool.

2) Next day add the other ingredients except the flowers, make up the must to 4.5 litres (8 pts) and ferment at 22°C (70°F). Add the flowers on the 3rd day.
3) On the 8th day, lightly press and strain the must into the fermenter and fit airlock. Whenever the ferment slows, feed the remaining honey in 113 g (4 oz) portions, adding the last amount a few days before racking (SG 1015).
4) Rack and add 2 sulphite tablets. Rack again as soon as the wine is really clear. Store at 10°C (50°F) for 2 years, racking and sulphiting (½ tablet) every 3rd month. Keep in bottle for another year at least before serving.

Beetroot wine *(sweet red after-dinner or blending wine)*

1585 g	washed, not peeled, beetroot	3½	lb
1360 g	granulated sugar	3	lb
450 ml	red grape concentrate	¾	pint
15 g	mixed dry spices (optional)	1	tbs
5 ml	each tartaric and citric acid	1	tsp
5 ml	grape tannin	1	tsp
5 ml	pectic enzyme	1	tsp
2.5 ml	starch enzyme	½	tsp
	super or Tokay yeast and nutrients		
	sulphite tablets		

1) Prepare yeast starter (see page 41). Dice the beetroot and in a large saucepan boil the pieces in 3.5 litres (6 pts) of water for about an hour until just tender. Place half the sugar and the spices in the mash-tun and strain the hot beetroot juice over the sugar, stirring until it has dissolved. When cool, add the concentrate, acids, tannin and 1 sulphite tablet and cover.
2) Next day, add the other ingredients except the remaining sugar and ferment at 22°C (70°F) for 3 days, stirring once daily.
3) Strain must into fermenter and fit airlock. Keep the vessel away from light or cover it with a dark cloth since the deep-red beetroot colour can easily turn brown. Whenever the ferment slows, feed the rest of the sugar in 113 g (4 oz) quantities, adding the last portion near the end of the fermentation (SG 1015–1020).
4) Rack and add 2 sulphite tablets. Rack again when the wine is really clear. Store covered or in a dark place at 10°C (50°F). Mature in bulk for 2 years, racking and sulphiting (½ tablet) every 3rd month. Store in bottle for another 9 months at least.

Carrot wine *(sweet white after-dinner or blending wine)*

2270 g	scrubbed, not peeled, carrots	5	lb
450 g	sultanas (or other dried fruit)	I	lb
1585 g	granulated sugar	3½	lb
5 ml	each tartaric and citric acid	I	tsp
5 ml	grape tannin	I	tsp
5 ml	pectic enzyme	I	tsp
2.5 ml	starch enzyme	½	tsp
	super or Tokay yeast and nutrients		
	sulphite tablets		

I) Prepare the yeast starter (see page 41). Slice the carrots and boil them in a large saucepan in 3 litres (5½ pts) of water for about an hour or until tender. Meanwhile mince the sultanas and place the puree with half the sugar in the mash-tun. Strain the hot carrot juice over the sugar and stir until it has dissolved. Cover and let cool.

2) Next day add the other ingredients except the rest of the sugar and ferment on the pulp at 22°C (70°F) for 10 days, stirring twice daily.

3) Lightly press the pulp and strain the juice into the fermenter. Fit airlock. Whenever the ferment slows, feed the rest of the sugar in 113 g (4 oz) quantities, adding the last portion just before racking (SG 1020–1025).

4) Rack and add 2 sulphite tablets. Rack again when the wine is really clear. Taste it and consider adding herbs or spices (see page 39). Store in bulk for 2 years, racking every 3rd month, and in bottle for another year before serving.

Tables

Conversion tables

The vital element in metric measures is the relation between solid weight and liquid volume. It is based on the fact that 1 litre water weighs precisely 1 kilo and would occupy a cube measuring 10 x 10 x 10 centimetres. This relationship is very useful when working out conversions in winemaking. All measures are approximate.

Weights

Metric into British:	British into metric:
1 kilo (1000 g) = 2 lb 3 oz	1 lb (16 oz) = 454 grammes
15 g = 1 tablespoon	1 oz = 28 grammes
5 g = 1 teaspoon	$\frac{1}{2}$ oz = 15 grammes (tablespoon)
	$\frac{1}{8}$ oz = 5 grammes (teaspoon)

Liquids

Metric into British:	British into metric:
1 litre (1000 ml) = 35 fl oz ($1\frac{3}{4}$ pt)	1 gallon (8 pts) = 4.54 litres
1 tablespoon (15 ml) = $\frac{1}{2}$ fl oz	1 pint (20 fl oz) = 568 ml
1 teaspoon (5 ml) = $\frac{1}{6}$ fl oz	1 fluid ounce = 28 ml

American (weights are the same as British, only liquid measures differ)

Metric into American:	American into metric:
1 litre (1000 ml) = 0.264 gallon	1 gallon (8 pts) = 3.785 litres
or $2\frac{1}{5}$ pints	1 pint (16 fl oz) = 0.473 litres
or 35 fl oz	1 fl oz = 28 ml
	1 tablespoon ($\frac{1}{2}$ fl oz) = 15 ml
	1 teaspoon ($\frac{1}{6}$ fl oz) = 5 ml

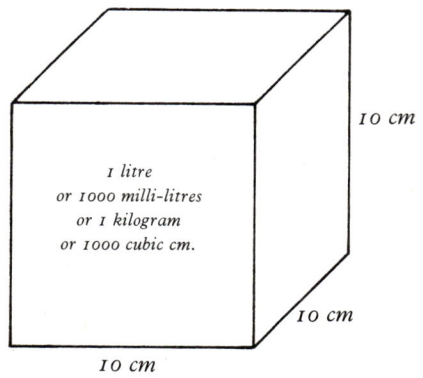

1 litre
or 1000 milli-litres
or 1 kilogram
or 1000 cubic cm.

10 cm
10 cm
10 cm

Temperature

Centi-grade		Fahrenheit
	0	32
	5	41
	10	50
	15	59
	20	68
	25	77
	30	86
	35	95
	40	104
	45	113
	50	122

Index